A BOATER'S
GUIDE
to VHF and GMDSS

The Boater's VHF Charter

Operating Your Marine VHF Radio

What to Do
- ✓ Identify your vessel.
- ✓ Listen before transmitting to avoid interference with other stations.
- ✓ Use accepted operating procedures.
- ✓ Replace your microphone or handset correctly when you have finished your call.
- ✓ Be polite and courteous.
- ✓ Be brief.
- ✓ Speak clearly.
- ✓ Monitor CH16 but use CH09 for calling other recreational vessels when possible.
- ✓ Use the lowest power that will enable communication to take place.
- ✓ Check out the correct channel to use before transmitting.

What Not to Do
- ⊘ Don't transmit false or misleading messages. The transmission of a false distress message is illegal.
- ⊘ Don't make long transmissions or hog a channel.
- ⊘ Don't operate your VHF radio in a manner that could endanger others or interfere with other radio users.
- ⊘ Don't use bad language.
- ⊘ Don't make repeated calls to a station that does not answer.

A BOATER'S GUIDE to VHF and GMDSS

Sue Fletcher

International Marine / McGraw-Hill

CAMDEN, MAINE • NEW YORK • CHICAGO • SAN FRANCISCO • LISBON
LONDON • MADRID • MEXICO CITY • MILAN • NEW DELHI • SAN JUAN
SEOUL • SINGAPORE • SYDNEY • TORONTO

International Marine

A Division of The McGraw-Hill Companies

10 9 8 7 6 5 4 3 2 1

Library of Congress Cataloging-in-Publication Data
Fletcher, Sue.
   A boater's guide to VHF and GMDSS / Sue Fletcher.
      p.   cm.
Includes index.
   ISBN 0-07-138802-8 (paperback)
   1. Radio on boats. 2. Shortwave radio. 3. Navigation—Safety measures. 4. Radio in navigation. 5. Artificial satellites in navigation. 6. Search and rescue operations. 7. Distress signals.
I. Title.
   VM325 .F58 2002
   623.89´32—dc21   2001008574

Questions regarding the content of this book should be addressed to
International Marine
P.O. Box 220
Camden, ME 04843
www.internationalmarine.com

Questions regarding the ordering of this book should be addressed to
The McGraw-Hill Companies
Customer Service Department
P.O. Box 547
Blacklick, OH 43004
Retail customers: 1-800-262-4729
Bookstores: 1-800-722-4726

This book is printed on 60# Computer Book by R.R. Donnelley
Design by Faith Hague
Page layout by Deborah Evans
Illustrations by Jim Sollers
Production by Janet Robbins
Edited by Jonathan Eaton, Dan Fales, and John Vigor

Contents

Foreword

I am pleased to have been invited to write the foreword for this new handbook, *A Boater's Guide to VHF and GMDSS*, which will fill a significant U.S. gap in affordable manuals to explain, in recreational boaters' terms, the fundamentals of the Global Maritime Distress and Safety System (GMDSS). The new GMDSS system was introduced in 1999 by the International Maritime Organization (IMO) as a major upgrade to the radio communications facilities prescribed for seagoing ships under the Safety of Life at Sea (SOLAS) Convention. The old system, based on manual Morse telegraphy with specialized radio officers, was essentially the original system mandated after the *Titanic* disaster. The old system, in addition to being labor-intensive, lacked global coverage and the benefits of modern automation techniques. The new GMDSS system incorporates the Inmarsat maritime satellite system and satellite emergency position-indicating radio beacons (EPIRBs), and adds automated techniques to the traditional maritime radio systems.

The GMDSS called for a major upgrade of communications facilities on large oceangoing ships of over 300 tons (272.16 metric tons) at some considerable expense. The U.S. Coast Guard was hard pressed to handle all aspects of the changeover, which included upgrading its own coastal radio networks to introduce the digital selective calling (DSC) automation techniques. The coast guard therefore decided to sponsor the U.S. GMDSS Implementation Task Force to assist in getting information to the maritime community. Although the task force was chartered by the U.S. Coast Guard, GMDSS implementation in Canada is very similar, and many Canadian authorities are represented on the task force. The task force has no regulatory authority but does make recommendations to appropriate authorities to resolve problems.

GMDSS also has important safety benefits for smaller craft, both to make their own distress alerts more efficient and reliable and also to communicate directly with larger ships when necessary. In the United States there are literally millions of private pleasure craft, or *voluntary* craft, that are permitted to use these new systems and (if using only the short-range VHF radio system) are not required to have station licenses or operator licenses. The task force has strongly advocated voluntary training for operators of the new VHF-DSC radios, both to ensure that the operators fully understand the procedures for their own safety and to ease the threat of excessive false alerts.

It is unfortunate that the U.S. Coast Guard was not able to upgrade its coastal VHF network for DSC by the February 1999 effective date for all GMDSS services. On the other hand, that delay has provided the task force with an opportunity to encourage such nongovernmental organizations as the U.S. Coast Guard Auxiliary and the U.S. Power Squadrons to incorporate GMDSS and VHF-DSC principles in their voluntary training programs. Another need cited by the task force was for an affordable, easy-to-understand GMDSS handbook to support such training and provide continuing reference and guidance for vessel operators. This book fills that need admirably and is available just as VHF-DSC radios are becoming widely available in the marketplace.

In summary, the U.S. GMDSS Task Force is pleased to endorse *A Boater's Guide to VHF and GMDSS* as a valuable aid throughout North America, especially for small-vessel operators, both to support the recommended training and for self-study purposes. It is important that all mariners understand the GMDSS, not just those serving on ships that are required to outfit for all GMDSS systems. To learn more about GMDSS, please visit the U.S. Coast Guard Web site, www/navcen.uscg.mil/marcomms/, or contact the GMDSS Task Force if you wish to receive GMDSS material (see appendix 7, Contact Information).

Captain Jack Fuechsel, USCG (Retired)
Director, U.S. GMDSS Task Force

Introduction

Radio communications have been used successfully by ships for more than a century. The latest evolution in commercial maritime communications is the Global Maritime Distress and Safety System (GMDSS), which uses digital selective calling (DSC). DSC introduces a level of automation to marine communications and reduces the need for a continual listening watch on calling channels. In 1912, the world learned about the *Titanic* disaster in the icy waters of the North Atlantic. Ships in the vicinity did not hear her distress calls because they were not required to listen on the radio 24 hours a day. Automatic watchkeeping has been a long time coming.

What do these developments in the world of big ships have to do with you, the operator of a small boat? Plenty, as it turns out. The analog (voice) marine VHF radio is about to undergo its biggest revolution since it was first used on boats, and its digital selective calling aspects will alter the way we call for help, report safety issues to the coast guard, call other vessels and make phone calls. *A Boater's Guide to VHF and GMDSS* is here to help you through the changes.

Because the changeover period is supposed to run until 2006, with both the new digital (DSC) and current analog (non-DSC, i.e., voice) systems functioning side-by-side until then, this book explains both systems. It is written entirely from a recreational boater's viewpoint to help you get the best from whichever system you use. DSC will have an increasing impact on the existing analog (voice) system, forcing changes that you will need to know about. So even if you don't have a state-of-the-art DSC radio yet, this book is still essential reading as changes occur in channel usage, calling up commercial ships, and calling for help. All these changes will alter the way you use your analog radio. Here, too, you will find tips on what to look for when you purchase a DSC radio.

About This Book

Having taught recreational sailors the principles and practice of VHF radio, I know that most boats would benefit from an on-call radio guru with a sense of humor, a wealth of explanations, and step-by-step instructions, to sit patiently at the elbow of the radio operator. This book is that guru.

The book's five parts are arranged to build your knowledge:

1. **Your VHF Radio** covers the current VHF system and GMDSS; DSC and non-DSC radios, and how to set them up; antennas and radio range; buying tips; and battery care.

2. **VHF Radio Protocol** looks at channel allocation; radio regulations and standard radio procedure; calling etiquette; and the phonetic alphabet.

3. **Using Your VHF Radio** explains how to get the most from your radio whether it's DSC or non-DSC. It covers distress, urgency, and safety calls; routine calls to other vessels and the coast guard; making a phone call; weather information; port operations and booking a marina berth; and red tape.

4. **The Global Maritime Distress and Safety System (GMDSS)** takes a more detailed look at the safety system and lists the reasons for the changes that are needed. It also covers recommended equipment; the use of EPIRBs and their registration; SARTs; and Navtex.

5. **Appendices** include maritime frequencies; broadcast schedules; contact information; a glossary; and a quick reference for making urgent calls.

Throughout the book practical examples are mingled with theoretical ideals, and the text is peppered with a host of tips and warnings, most from my personal, recreational boating experience. Everything is written in plain English, and where jargon is unavoidable I have explained it either in the text or as individual points identified as *Geek-Speak*. (Note that throughout the book, *miles* refers to nautical miles; statute miles, when given, are always referred to as *statute miles*.) This book aims to introduce you to VHF radio, both digital and analog, in the easiest way possible.

What this book doesn't try to do is make you a telecommunications expert: in the same way that you don't need to know how electricity is generated in order to plug in your TV, you don't need to know how antennas work to use a VHF radio.

There are several ways to use this book. First, there is the cover-to-cover approach, which is the best way to wring every last drop out of its content and get a good night's sleep in the bargain. On the other hand, if you just want to dip into it, you'll find this book completely user-friendly. The table of contents lists topics in each section so you can find a subject fast, but you can also refer to the detailed index.

Just in case you forget how to make a particular call, the vital information is condensed into a Quick Reference as appendix 9, close to the back of the book where you'll be able to find it speedily. After all, this book is designed to work as your personal radio guru, straight from the locker, no battery needed.

Acknowledgments

I would like to thank the following people for their help, advice, and encouragement during the research and writing of this book. My grateful thanks go to: Jack Fuechsel, director of the U.S. GMDSS Task Force, for his enthusiasm and endless supply of useful contacts, as well as for taking the time to write the foreword for the book; Joe Hersey and Ed Brady, U.S. Coast Guard; Richard Swanson, Federal Communications Commission; Jim Tindall, Maritel; Andy Nelson, Canadian Coast Guard; John Nosotti, Industry Canada; Peter Ryan, Ryan & Associates, Vancouver; and John P. Stohrer, Raymarine, Inc.

PART 1

YOUR
VHF RADIO

CHAPTER 1

Overview of the VHF-DSC System

Before the days of radio for marine communications, a vessel hoisted a series of flags, sailed out of port and, unless she returned to port, nothing was known about her whereabouts or misfortune. The introduction and subsequent evolution of marine radio over the past hundred years has helped considerably in reducing the number of losses, but it isn't perfect and vessels still go missing. This is why the International Maritime Organization (IMO), the body that regulates shipping, deemed it necessary to implement a complete overhaul of maritime communications. The new system is called the Global Maritime Distress and Safety System, more commonly known as GMDSS (a full explanation of the system is given in chapter 21).

One or more radios have always been at the heart of the maritime communications system. Until the 1960s, the only marine radio in general use was capable of transmitting over very long distances using medium frequency (MF) or high frequency (HF) radio waves. The technology on which this radio is based gives rise to their generic name of *single-sideband* or SSB radios. However, the dramatic increase in the numbers of commercial and recreational boats during the 1960s and 1970s brought about a requirement for an additional short-range radio that couldn't hog a channel over thousands of miles. Hence the development of a radio that uses very high frequencies (VHF). Both SSB and VHF radios are based on technology that only allows voice messages and is known as *analog communication.*

Into these analog systems has been integrated another technology that uses the ones and zeros of digital codes to transmit numerical data such as vessel identification numbers, latitude, and longitude. A radio that has this capability is known as a Digital Selective Calling (DSC) radio; both SSB and VHF radios can have DSC capability.

Recreational craft that stay within 20 miles of the coast only need to carry the short-range VHF radio. Therefore, all technical discussions in the book apply to VHF radios only, unless otherwise stated.

Why Digital Selective Calling?

Digital selective calling provides a means of automating most radio calls, which makes your marine radio almost as easy to use as your telephone. This analogy to the telephone is especially appropriate because DSC, in effect, provides you with a digital tone-dialing system. This means you can selectively call another *station* directly, rather than transmitting a general message to all stations in the hope that the one you want is listening.

Each radio station is allocated a unique nine-digit number, known as the Maritime Mobile Service Identity (MMSI) number. This number works the same way a telephone number does, and is used to alert one individual vessel, a defined group of vessels, or a coast station. In the case of distress, urgency, and safety calls, all vessels and coast stations within receiving distance are alerted.

Once digital contact has been made (the equivalent on land of picking up the telephone receiver), calls continue by analog (voice) communication in just the same way that they do now, so it is no problem for a DSC radio to communicate by voice with a non-DSC radio. The same voice channels are used by both analog only and DSC VHF radios, so if you want to use your DSC radio to hail a marina for a berth for the night, you talk on the same channel as you would on an analog radio.

> ## Geek-Speak
>
> Don't think "AM/FM stereo broadcast radio" when you see the terms *radio station*, *coast station*, *ship station*, or even just *station* in a nautical context. All these terms refer to the radio equipment on any vessel or at any land post, and by extension to the vessel or land post itself.

Unlike the telephone signal, the DSC digital dialing signal is capable of carrying other information, such as your vessel's identity (MMSI number), the vessel's position, the nature of the call, and the information specifying the channel for the subsequent voice communications. The complete message is transmitted in one quick burst that takes less than one second to send, thus reducing the demand for time on the calling channel.

When the call is received by the other party, an alarm sounds and details of the calling station are displayed on the screen, and, in case the call goes unanswered, these details are stored in the Received Calls log. If the call is picked up immediately by the receiving station, the DSC radio will automatically retune to the analog working channel for the follow-on voice communications.

The Ray 45 (top) is a regular VHF radio for voice communications only. The Ray 53 (bottom) has both voice and DSC capabilities and meets FCC SC 101 requirements: in a distress situation the covered distress button (on the microphone on this model) can be activated to transmit a digital alert that contains the identity and position of the distressed vessel. (Raymarine Inc.)

Another characteristic that the DSC radio has in common with the telephone is that you no longer need to select the channel the digital signal is sent on: the equipment does that for you. The digital information is automatically transmitted on VHF channel 70 (CH70), which has been internationally allocated only for use with DSC. On older, non-DSC radios, voice communications are still possible—though illegal—on CH70. On DSC radios, voice transmissions have been disabled on CH70.

The automation of the front-end digital signal and its automatic reception and storage mean that radio watchkeeping is now also automatic. You do not actually have to listen to CH70, so it doesn't matter if you miss the alarm call because the details are stored in the radio's Received Calls log for later recall. When everyone has a DSC radio this will leave you free to continue your boating without having to listen constantly in case your vessel is being hailed or another vessel has run into a problem.

The most important aspect of the change to digital selective calling is that it gives everyone who uses it the ability to call for help automatically at the touch of a button. The digital signal can carry the vessel's identity, its position, the time the vessel was at that position, and the nature of the problem. Once the digital call is acknowledged by the coast guard, voice communications take over, so that more details of the problem can be given, such as the number of people on board. But remember, the coast guard will not be able to monitor VHF-DSC calls for a few more years, though there are some coast guard cutters that can do so now.

Although digital signals can travel up to 20 percent farther than analog signals, the distance at which a VHF signal can be detected is determined by whether the antennas of the transmitting and sending stations can "see" each other (see page 22). Therefore, for a vessel's VHF-DSC radio to receive digital messages from a coastal station, it must be within about 50 miles of the coast. Though the DSC part of the radio may send and receive signals over 50 miles, the realistic range of all other channels in your VHF radio may only be 10 to 20 miles. When you're boating beyond 50 miles, it's wise to carry an SSB radio that uses both medium frequency (MF) and high-frequency (HF) radio signals.

How Long before I Need to Buy a New Radio?

Because of the change to the GMDSS system, the United States Coast Guard (USCG) has underway a national program of fitting VHF-DSC shoreside facilities, with completion due by 2006. As a recreational boater who uses VHF radio, you'll have to decide by then whether to change your current analog VHF radio for one with digital selective calling. Bear in mind, however, that no regulations *force* recreational boaters to carry any form of radio equipment, which will also hold true in the foreseeable future for a DSC radio.

The present analog VHF radio system relies entirely on voice communication. If you get into trouble and need to call for help, you do so on channel 16 (CH16). This channel is monitored 24 hours a day by the coast guard, by most commercial ships in coastal waters, and, under international regulations, by recreational boaters when they are on the water and have their radios switched on. As there is no automatic radio watchkeeping feature on CH16, each station must physically maintain a listening watch at all times if your distress call is to be received. Under international rules, ships will monitor CH16 for distress calls until at least the year 2005, and probably longer than that.

By now you're probably asking yourself, "Why do I need to know anything about a system I can choose not to use?" Here's why.

- Any marine radio must be approved for use in U.S. waters by the Federal Communications Commission (FCC). From 1999 on, all marine radio transmitters submitted for FCC type acceptance in the United States must have some form of DSC capability. Although *current* radio models can continue to be manufactured, *new* models must have DSC; so if you change your radio in the future, it will almost certainly be DSC-capable.
- The upgrade of coast guard VHF communications from their current analog-only system to one with DSC will encourage the sale of radios with DSC capability.
- As more DSC radios are manufactured, prices will fall. By early 2002, prices were already a third lower than they were in 1999.
- As increasing numbers of recreational craft change to DSC, fewer craft will be listening on CH16, which will reduce the chances of a CH16 distress call being heard.
- Commercial ships will continue their VHF CH16 watchkeeping for the foreseeable future, but as time goes on, current analog VHF and SSB radios will begin to become obsolete.

Benefits of Using DSC

As long as the coast guard continues a listening watch on CH16 and you are within 20 miles or so of the coast, making a call on your existing radio has as much chance of being heard as it always has. So, as a recreational boater you may question the necessity to fit new equipment before your current VHF radio is beyond repair, but the arguments for doing so are persuasive:

- In an emergency, you can send at the touch of a button the identity of your vessel, a precise position, and the nature of your distress. The alert will be automatically repeated every four minutes or so until an acknowledgment is received, leaving you free to continue bailing, fighting the fire, or whatever else you need to do to tackle the problem. Position can be input automatically or manually when a GPS or loran is connected to the radio.

    Once the DSC alert is received, all further communication is carried out by voice on CH16 in the usual way if you are within range.

- The precise position your radio sends with the alert takes the "search" out of "search and rescue," so you should be found more quickly. The coast guard considers getting an identity and a position fix to be a significant advantage of DSC.

- Digital signals are quicker to send than voice (analog) signals. In distress situations, particularly on small vessels where damage to the radio, batteries, or antenna is likely, the functioning time of the radio may be limited. During this time, the speed with which a DSC distress alert can be transmitted and received makes it more likely to bring you the help you need than a longer voice distress call would.

- It will make day-to-day radio operating much easier because calling is automatic and you will no longer need to keep a permanent listening watch on CH16. An alarm will ring when you are being called, or when an emergency is declared by another vessel, so the rest of the time you can get on with enjoying your boating.

- It is a worldwide system that can be used anywhere, and because it is automatic it avoids possible language barriers.

- All big ships can respond instantly to DSC calls. From 2003–4, the Canadian Coast Guard will be able to respond; and from 2005–6, the U.S. Coast Guard may be fully equipped for VHF-DSC operations. The Coast Radio Station service, which has been unavailable for several years, is undergoing an upgrading program that will include a VHF-DSC CH70 watch. As stations come back into service,

Handsets and speakers that are waterproof and designed to be used away from the main unit are particularly useful in vessels with different helming and navigation positions. Some models allow you to use up to three waterproof cellular-type handsets and speakers in other locations. (Raymarine Inc.)

they will monitor CH70 for distress alerts and relay them to the coast guard.

The GMDSS is not perfect for the recreational boater because it was designed for use by commercial shipping worldwide. But throughout this book you'll find suggestions for the best ways to overcome its imperfections.

CHAPTER 2

Non-DSC VHF Radios

The non-DSC VHF radio is the analog (voice) radio we all currently use and are familiar with. Most fixed radios used on boats today are relatively sophisticated units that have many features, as opposed to the older crystal-controlled sets that had just two radio channels, CH16 and CH06. A modern radio, with 145 send and/or receive channels is based on technology that allows many more functions to be packed into smaller spaces. At first glance these functions may not be particularly self-explanatory, so below is a simple guide to the most commonly found features and ways they may be labeled.

CHANNEL 16 DEDICATED BUTTON: CH16, 16, or EMER. This is the primary channel for calling the coast guard and passing distress and urgency messages by voice. Channel 16 is also used for calling other vessels and

Radio Panel of a Non-DSC VHF Radio. Although this Ray 210 model is no longer made, it is representative of many full-featured, non-DSC radios still in use. (Raymarine Inc.)

7

coast stations. When you press the CH16 button, the radio will automatically tune to CH16. Ideally, it should also select high power automatically (see Power Switch below) For more detailed information on the use of CH16, see pages 46–47.

This button may be labeled "16/9," in which case it accesses both CH16 and CH09. Channel 9 can be an alternative calling channel for recreational craft (see chapter 10).

CHANNEL SELECTOR. This may be in the form of a rotating knob, up-down switches, or a numeric keypad.

DIM or a **light symbol.** Background illumination for keys and/or display.

DISTANT/LOCAL: D/L. Desensitizes the receiver in high noise and/or high traffic areas. This feature reduces pager and cellular phone tower interference.

DUAL WATCH: DW. This allows you to monitor CH16 and one other channel simultaneously without having to switch manually between them. Transmitting should not be possible when dual watch is activated. On most units, when the transmit switch is pressed or the handset is lifted from its storage hook, dual watch is automatically switched off and the radio tunes to the optional channel, not CH16. This prevents calls from being transmitted over CH16 by mistake. If you want to select CH16, push the dedicated CH16 button.

DUAL WATCH WEATHER: DWX. Same as Dual Watch but monitors the last selected weather channel, as well. Used to implement automatic Weather Alert feature.

FUNCTION: FUNC. Allows you to access secondary functions of the unit.

INTERNATIONAL/U.S.: INT/U.S. Allows you to select channels from the U.S. Maritime Bandplan (U.S.) or the International Bandplan (INT). Some radios will have this as a menu option rather than as a button. Channels with an A designation, such as Ch22A, are available in the U.S. and Canadian Bandplans. In the International Bandplan, CH22 uses different frequencies.

MEMORY and **SCAN.** These functions could be labeled any of the following: **PSCN, PSC, MS, SCN, SS SCAN, SC SCAN, R/D, TAG, CALL, MEM, M+, M−, CLR.** These two features allow you to monitor and program into the radio's memory any number of channels you wish. The scanner sequentially moves from one channel to the next, stopping where a signal is detected. The radio manufacturer's handbook will give detailed instructions about the use of all these buttons.

MEMORY RECALL: RCL. Displays in turn all the channels currently stored in memory.

MICROPHONE and **PRESS TO TRANSMIT SWITCH: MIC** and **PTT.** When you press the PTT switch on the side or back of the microphone, your radio becomes a transmitter that allows your speech to be broadcast. When you release the switch, the radio reverts to being a receiver and you listen. The PTT switch, for safety reasons, cannot be locked in transmit mode. When the microphone is not in use, store it where the PTT switch can't be accidentally pressed; otherwise you'll be broadcasting the sounds of life aboard to everyone within radio range. Our crowded anchorage was once entertained for half an hour by the skipper and mate discussing the impending visit of the mate's mother—definitely not ship's business! Of greater concern is if the radio is tuned to CH16, which may jam the channel for many miles around. Some radios come with a "time-out" feature that automatically returns the radio to receive after five minutes of continuous transmitting.

Tip Fit a hook or cradle to hold the microphone firmly in place when it's not in use.

POWER SWITCH: HI/LO, 25/1. The maximum power output for a U.S. or Canadian VHF radio is 25 watts (25 W) and is used for distress and urgency communications and calls to the coast guard, as well as to other boats.

Low power, 1 watt (1 W), should be selected in all other circumstances to avoid undue interference with other stations (see Capture Effect, pages 34–35). Channels 17 and 77 are restricted to 1 W only, but on any other channel you can choose the power.

QUICK-ACCESS KEYS: M1, M2, M3, etc. Quick-access keys that allow you to program in specific working or weather channels. Most are set the same way you would a car radio: tune the radio to the desired channel and press and hold the desired M key.

SQUELCH CONTROL: SQ, SQLCH. The squelch control cuts out background hiss and requires that an incoming signal be of a specific strength to be heard. If it's turned too far up it will cut out altogether the signal you're listening for.

TRANSMITTING INDICATOR: TX. A red light-emitting diode or TX sign will light up on the display when you are transmitting.

VOLUME and **ON/OFF: VOL** and **ON/OFF.** The On/Off switch is usually incorporated in the volume-control knob, and a light indicates that the unit is switched on.

VOLTAGE: VOLT. Displays the detected input voltage.

WEATHER CHANNELS: WX1, WX2, etc. Dedicated weather channels. Receive only. More on this in chapter 16, Weather Information.

CHAPTER 3

Portable Radios

For small open boats, a portable radio is almost the only choice. A portable, or handheld, may also be used as a back-up to a fixed unit and because it is a completely self-contained unit it will work when the vessel has been dismasted or if the main electrical supply has failed.

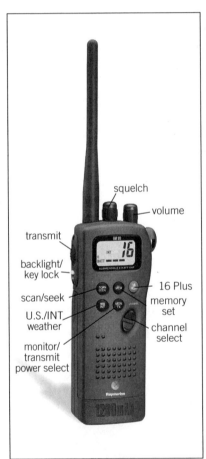

squelch

volume

transmit

backlight/
key lock

scan/seek

U.S./INT
weather

monitor/
transmit
power select

16 Plus

memory
set

channel
select

Non-DSC Portable VHF Radio. The Ray 106 is available in models that accommodate either alkaline or rechargeable batteries. (Raymarine Inc.)

At the time of writing, digital selective calling handheld radios are beginning to appear on the market. Confusingly, there are also portable units sold as "GMDSS Transportables," but these radios are meant for merchant ships; they have a limited number of channels and require special batteries that can't be recharged. They are generally colored a bright orange or yellow and *do not have a DSC capability*. They are intended for use in survival craft in emergencies when it's desirable to have a portable radio to communicate with the rescue craft during the final stages of the rescue. Search-and-rescue transponders (SARTs) also guide rescuers to you (see chapter 22, Other GMDSS Equipment).

The most useful kind of portable radio incorporates a global positioning system (GPS) receiver, so that your vessel's position will be included automatically in any distress alert—some may be on the market soon. Without GPS, the DSC features are rendered relatively useless because a portable radio is unlikely to be permanently connected to an external GPS unit. You'll need good onboard discipline to keep your position constantly updated. If you take a non-GPS DSC radio to a life raft, the position information will rapidly become unreliable, and after 23½ hours (the limit of the radio's memory) the position will be erased.

Compared with a fixed unit, any handheld radio suffers three disadvantages: low transmitting power, low antenna height, and limited battery capacity. Let's take each disadvantage in turn.

Low transmitting power: High power in a handheld is 5 or 6 W compared to 25 W on a fixed unit. This is to preserve battery power. You can increase the effective output of the radio by up to 40 percent by transmitting through a high-gain masthead antenna, but only if the antenna is vertical. The big problem is that these antennas are about 8 feet (2.4 m) long and only work well when upright. So if you have a small sailboat that spends most of its sea time heeled far over, this option is not for you.

Low antenna height: Because of the line-of-sight characteristic of a VHF radio signal, its range is determined antenna height for both sending and receiving. Two handhelds 6 feet above the water have a range of approximately 5 miles. A masthead antenna can double this distance (see illustration page 22).

Limited battery capacity: Transmitting consumes battery power faster than a monkey can down peanuts, and most handheld radios yield around 30 minutes of talk time on full power. This can be significantly increased by

- using low power (1 W) whenever possible. It is good for at least 2 miles.
- not wasting time calling other vessels on channels 09 or 16 but calling direct on an agreed working channel
- keeping calls brief and not repeating words
- ensuring you're understood the first time by speaking clearly in plain English
- planning what you're going to say before pressing the button. "Ums" and "Uhs" eat battery power.
- choosing equipment that uses regular alkaline cells. These are readily available and can be kept on board and remain fully charged until required. If there's a generator aboard, you can select a rechargeable type. For an open boat, select a handheld that's at least waterproof if not classified as "submersible."

These problems can be overcome, but if your boat allows it, opt for a fixed unit, which delivers more features, more transmitting power, more talk time, and a greater range. But even after you have obtained a fixed unit it's still a good idea to have at least one portable radio, which can offer these advantages:

- It can be used in the vessel's tender for communications with the primary vessel.
- The reduced radio range is less likely to cause interference with other radio users.
- It can be used in a distress situation to speak to rescuers.

CHAPTER 4

VHF-DSC Radios

A digital selective calling (DSC) radio can be regarded as a combination of a telephone and a traditional marine VHF radio. DSC acts like the keypad and bell of a telephone, allowing you to call direct and "ring" other DSC radios, or allow others to call you, without having to listen to a speaker. If you can't answer the call, the details are stored in the Received Calls log. The DSC radio also allows you to send a formatted distress alert, a Mayday, instantly to any other DSC radios in your local area, and at some future time, to the coast guard.

There is a range of options available for DSC units: the appropriate choice for you depends on whether or not you must comply with the IMO's GMDSS regulations and, as recreational boaters, most of you won't need to. Your interest will center around short-range VHF-DSC radios instead of the long-range single-sideband (SSB) tranceivers.

Geek-Speak

The "DSC Controller" is the user interface that controls the DSC elements of the VHF transceiver. We retain the term because many DSC units show it in the display (see photo page 19). Some controllers are separate from the radio; others are integrated into it.

Equipment Classes

The International Telecommunication Union (ITU) determines the specifications for and categorizes VHF-DSC equipment by the type of vessel and the radio's ultimate usage. It differentiates between equipment specifications using classifications A, B, and D. Class C has been withdrawn.

The equipment class that a vessel must carry is determined by the distance the vessel travels from the shore. Vessels that travel more than 150 miles offshore carry class A equipment, vessels that travel more than 50 miles but less than 150 miles offshore carry class B, and vessels that remain within 50 miles of the coast carry class D. Each class is explained in more detail below.

Class A SSB and VHF equipment is carried by ships that travel in all sea areas and have both medium-frequency (MF) and high-frequency (HF) long-range radio installations. This equipment fully complies with all the requirements of the GMDSS but offers no particular benefit for recreational craft, with the exception of flexibility and operational convenience.

Class B equipment is required for vessels that travel within 150 miles of the shore and are not required to carry class A equipment. These vessels carry SSB-MF and VHF radios to comply with the minimum requirements of the GMDSS.

Class D equipment is intended to provide minimum DSC capability for VHF use within 50 miles of the shore. It doesn't necessarily meet all the requirements of the GMDSS. Most manufacturers have a range of radios within this class for recreational boating use. Class D radios have two receivers—one for DSC only, the other for normal voice operations.

SC 101 is a standard devised by U.S. authorities to ensure that there will be a VHF-DSC radio to suit everyone's finances. This specification produces truly budget-priced DSC capabilities, and there may be significant restrictions to the features provided, such as

- no screen to display messages. This means it's impossible to show an incoming call, and without being able to see the menu, the operator will be severely handicapped.
- no numeric keypad. This makes it difficult to make a routine DSC call using an MMSI number, since the input mechanism is similar to that used in programming a digital watch. Try doing that while beating to windward in a Force 6 wind!
- a reduced call menu. However, this allows the transmission and reception of distress calls and the automatic update of position and time.
- only one radio receiver. This makes it impossible for the radio to listen on CH70 for a coast guard DSC acknowledgment to a distress call while simultaneously listening on CH16 for a response by voice. Some transceivers offer a scan feature designed to detect digital calls on CH70, and an analog call on any other desired channel, but this is not a required feature for the SC 101 radio.

Recreational craft are voluntary users of radio, which means that you can elect to fit any class of DSC radio you choose, or not bother at all. Since this book is written primarily for recreational boaters, it concentrates on the class D DSC radio and the SC 101 radio—both were designed with the recreational boater in mind.

Regardless of the sophistication of the radio you buy, you do need some explanation of the controls commonly found on VHF-DSC marine radios. Refer to chapter 2, Non-DSC VHF Radios, for those features common to both DSC and non-DSC radios.

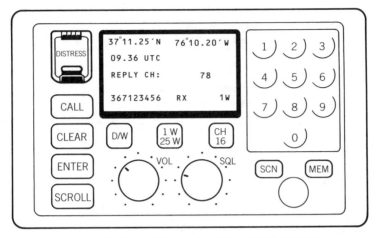

Schematic of a Typical Recreational Craft VHF-DSC Radio

VHF-DSC Radio Controls and Functions

The accompanying illustration of a typical recreational craft VHF-DSC radio and the following explanation of the DSC functions give a general overview of what you're likely to encounter. Individual manufacturers interpret the specification differently, just as the manufacturers of existing radios do, and there may be additional features not shown here. *This chapter is no substitute for reading your radio operator's handbook.*

DISPLAY. This should be large and easy to read by day and night, particularly if you wear reading glasses. The physical size of the radio is likely to determine this. The screen will display the following.

- the menu and instructions
- a position derived from the vessel's GPS or loran (if fitted). *Position is transmitted automatically only in a distress alert.* When you're using the DSC controller to transmit *urgency, safety,* or *routine traffic* (see glossary), position is *not* automatically included in the data unless the radio is specially programmed to do so.
- time in Universal Coordinated Time (UTC), previously known as Greenwich Mean Time (GMT). To convert local time, see the UTC entry in the glossary.
- the vessel's MMSI number (see the following section)
- the power level selected: 1 W low power or 25 W high power
- incoming and received calls
- transmission (TX) or reception (RX) mode
- automatic retransmit mode when sending a distress alert. When no distress acknowledgment is received, the equipment will automatically retransmit the alert randomly between 3 ½ and 4 ½ minutes from the beginning of the previous alert.

DISTRESS button. This clearly identifiable red button is the radio's most noted feature. It allows you to transmit an automatic DSC distress alert, known as a *Mayday*. To prevent accidental operation it is guarded by a spring-loaded cover. (Using the distress button correctly is covered in chapter 11, Distress Traffic.)

Geek-Speak

"Traffic" refers to radio communications.

Menu/CALL button. This gives you access to the DSC controller menu, which will offer some or all of the following:

- **Individual call.** You can call just one other specific station using a number (an MMSI) you enter on the keypad or take from a directory.
- **All ships.** Your *urgency*, *safety*, or *routine* call (see glossary) will go to all other DSC-equipped stations.
- **Received Calls log.** This is an automatic log of calls received.
- **Other.** This function allows you to maintain your directory, manually enter position and time, program a single number that will reach a group of stations (see page 28 on group MMSI numbers), and test the radio unit.

CANCEL/CLEAR button. This switches off the digital aspect of the unit so that you can use regular voice communications. The DSC display will continue to show position, time, MMSI number, and the channel number in use. The "cancel" function will act automatically after five minutes of inactivity on the DSC controller.

ENTER. You press this to enter, confirm, or send a selected menu item.

SCROLL ⇕. This allows you to scroll through the menu. When you scroll to the item you want, press **ENTER** to select it.

DUPLEX. This feature uses a piece of electronics to receive and transmit simultaneously on two antennas to make it possible to hold a normal conversation over the land-based phone system. A half or semiduplex radio needs only one antenna but there can be no simultaneous conversations. It's a transmit then receive system.

Geek-Speak

Remember: a *ship station* is the radio equipment on a vessel and a *coast station* is land-based radio equipment.

The hierarchical menu structure of a typical class D DSC radio is shown in the illustration next page. The basic SC 101 radio won't have all these options, whereas top-end equipment may have more.

The diagram illustrates which calls are likely to be available to you on a typical VHF-DSC radio. *Do not, however, use the diagram as a substitute for reading the operator's handbook that comes with your radio:* the labeling and the way features work might differ on your radio.

As soon as the unit is switched on, you can use it for voice calls. To make a Mayday call using DSC, press the DISTRESS button once to get the distress menu. The default DSC call is undesignated, but you can scroll through the more descriptive call menu illustrated to transmit a more specific message if you have time.

For all other DSC calls, press the CALL button. This will offer you the Call and Other Functions menus as illustrated.

A DSC radio based on the SC 101 specification will have the following minimum features:

- the ability to automatically transmit an "Undesignated" distress alert, an MMSI number, a position, and the time in UTC (see glossary), and receive an acknowledgment to its alert
- the ability to transmit an "All Ships" call
- the ability to transmit a routine call to an "Individual Station"
- automatic selection of a voice channel for communications when an "All Ships" call or a call to an "Individual Station" is selected
- the ability to receive a "Distress" alert, an "All Ships" call, and a call from an "Individual Station"

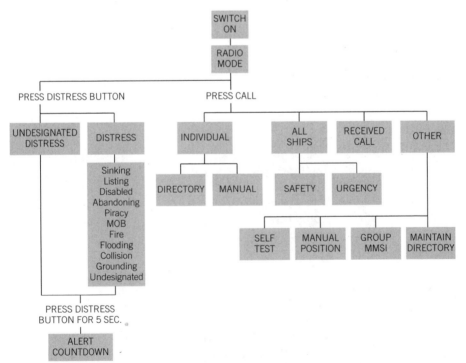

Menu Structure of the Typical Class D DSC Controller

Maritime Mobile Service Identity (MMSI) Numbers

When you buy new DSC equipment it must be programmed with a nine-digit Maritime Mobile Service Identity (MMSI) number. Some radios will not operate in DSC mode without an MMSI number keyed in. MMSI numbers are allocated to individual vessels, to groups of vessels, and to shore posts.

Using the telephone-number function on DSC-equipped radios, you can call coast guard stations, other DSC-equipped vessels, and other DSC-equipped shoreside facilities, and they can selectively call you. In the event of distress, the dedicated button allows you to make a DSC distress alert that automatically transmits your MMSI number, your position, and the time the position was valid. It will be received by any VHF-DSC-equipped coast guard station or ship within your radio range. Although a few DSC controllers will work without an MMSI number programmed into the unit, most of the benefit of DSC is lost without its inclusion. Without an MMSI number, no other vessel will be able to contact you and more importantly, if you get into trouble, the coast guard will not have your identity, and so won't know which boat to look for.

How to Get an MMSI Number

In the United States, contact BoatU.S., Maritel, or Sea Tow for an identity number (see appendix 7, Contact Information). They are authorized to issue MMSI numbers to recreational boaters.

In Canada all requests for MMSI numbers must be made through the Industry Canada Web site (see appendix 7 at Industry Canada, Victoria District Office). Print the Maritime Mobile Service Identities Client Procedures Circular and fill out the relevant "Annex(es)" (forms). Fax or mail the completed form(s) to the nearest district office or to the Victoria District office. Contact information for district offices is given in circular RIC-66, also available on the Web site. There is no provision for any other means of MMSI application.

In use, the system is very much like the land-based telephone service. DSC simply provides a digital start to voice communication by calling another DSC radio and waiting for it to be answered. In the called vessel or station an alarm sounds, thus offering automatic watchkeeping. On anything but the most basic radio, unanswered calls are stored in the "Received Calls" log for later retrieval.

All MMSI numbers are nine digits and have at least two components: a three-digit national or country code (known as an *MID*), and an individual station identify code (coast station ID codes are four digits and ship station ID codes are six digits). Coast stations have an additional, two-digit 00 prefix.

The United States has several national codes for use by recreational craft. They are: 366, 367, 368, 379, 559, 303, 338, and 358. The Canadian code is 316.

17

An example of a *ship station* MMSI is

MID (national code): 367
Individual station identity: 123456
Complete MMSI number: 367123456

An example of a *coast station* MMSI is

Shore station code: 00
MID (national code): 367
Individual station identity: 1234
Complete MMSI number: 003671234

Geek-Speak

The national or country code portion of the MMSI number is known as an "MID" (Maritime Identification Digits). MID codes are assigned by the ITU for use in various maritime areas.

The MMSI numbers of U.S. and Canadian Coast Guard stations are listed in appendix 6.

The MMSI number allows you to make automatic calls through your DSC equipment, and your equipment transmits this identity number when you are in distress.

Your vessel's identity number may be programmed into a new radio if you have already been assigned the number and order the radio that way from the supplier. In that case, the registration database will have all the information needed to assist you when you're in distress. If you have not been assigned an MMSI, you must obtain the number from the BoatU.S., Maritel, or Sea Tow MMSI Web sites for unlicensed vessels. (Also check with the U.S. Coast Guard.) Once you have the number arrange for it to be programmed into your radio. Failure to do so negates the special advantages of DSC if you get into trouble and need to be rescued.

The MMSI number, like the voice call sign, is a unique identifier for the vessel and the owner. If you sell the vessel, contact the MMSI provider so they can update the database. Likewise, if you upgrade to a new radio and sell your old DSC unit, erase the MMSI number before turning it over to the new owner.

Tip If your DSC is owner-programmable, check with your DSC handbook for the number of attempts you have to enter the MMSI number correctly. Some units allow only two attempts, so if you misprogram the MMSI both times, you may have to return the DSC unit to the supplier.

Radio Buyer's Clinic

Buying a new radio is not a decision to be made without some thought. Before you finally purchase your radio, consider the following points and write down your exact requirements. This will give you a more effective guide to the radio you need and help you avoid falling for the unit the salesperson wants to unload on you. Here are some points to consider:

- Do you want to use DSC? If you're buying a new radio, it's more cost-effective to buy one already fitted with DSC (see accompanying photo) or one that can have a DSC controller added at a later date (see photo on page 3).
- Not all DSC units are the same. Buying the cheapest one will give you little more than the ability to send a distress call. Consider carefully the features you want.
- If you currently do not own a GPS receiver or loran, consider buying one if you decide to purchase a DSC-equipped radio; otherwise, your position has to be manually updated. Some DSC models have an integrated GPS receiver.
- What available features do you want? Options might include direct dialing into the phone network and an extension handset for use in the cockpit.
- How waterproof should the radio be?
- Is the DISTRESS button protected with a spring-loaded cover? All transceivers approved by the FCC have this feature.
- How easy is it to read and use the menu?
- How comprehensive and comprehensible is the owner's manual?

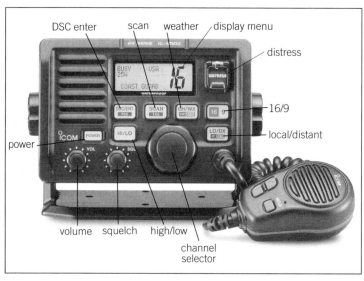

This Icom 502 VHF DSC radio has a built-in DSC controller. (Icom U.K.)

- Does the radio have a text function? This is useful for retrieving MMSI numbers from the directory.
- If the radio lacks a dedicated CH70 receiver, does it have an effective CH70 scan feature?
- Does the radio come with a cradle for the microphone?
- Can you select from a number of alarm options? Most electronics on board your boat have at least one alarm each. A piece of equipment that makes its own alarms easy to identify is worth considering.
- Are there different microphone options available, for example, a fist type and a handset type?
- What space do you have? Take measurements of the surface and depth available.
- If the radio is to be mounted on a bulkhead, can the space behind the bulkhead take the transceiver without tangling with other wires or bending its own wiring through dangerous angles?
- Is the display easy and clear to read? About a third of adults need reading glasses, and a display that is readable without their use is a bonus.
- Is the numeric keypad suitable for cold, wet fingers on hands as dexterous as a baseball glove?
- Can the radio be back-lit at night, and how bright is the light? The loss of night sight is an important factor often overlooked by manufacturers. Is there a dimmer? Does adjusting the back-lighting require pushing one button (preferred) or two buttons, or do you need to consult a menu?
- How well can the display be read in bright sunshine? Some displays disappear almost completely.
- Are switches easy to find and use at night?
- How easy is the radio to install, and could a long run of wire cause a voltage drop, and therefore problems with the unit? It is generally accepted that a voltage drop of 0.3–0.5 volts between the battery and the radio is the maximum acceptable. Measure this with a voltmeter while the radio is transmitting.
- How easy is the radio to use? Will you need to ask your six-year-old nephew to help you find the On/Off switch?

CHAPTER 5

Radio Installation

Where to Situate the Radio

Your marine radio must be fixed in a convenient position where you can use and read the controls easily, particularly at night. The screen may be illuminated, but are the rest of the controls easy to locate? Cold, wet fingers, and tired eyes are not compatible with microsized buttons, and if the radio is placed where it's difficult to see what you're doing, finding CH16 will be like looking for a black cat in a dark room. The radio must be sited away from heat, the steering compass, the engine, sea spray, and dampness, and be well secured. The installation manual should indicate the minimum safe distance from the compass to fit the radio; otherwise, it's likely to cause deviation.

Unless the radio is guaranteed to be absolutely waterproof, it must be located somewhere dry, usually the cabin on a small boat. In order to hear it while you're in the cockpit, it's wise to fit a waterproof speaker close to the helm but not next to the steering compass. This allows the watchkeeper to monitor the radio without disturbing the sleeping crew below and keeps the skipper in touch with communications while he or she is on deck. An extension microphone handset may be required in cases like these. In a powerboat, an external speaker provides good volume over engine noise.

Antenna

The antenna is the device that sends the radio transmission into the air and receives answers. To get the most dependable results from your radio installation, buy the best-quality antenna, coaxial cable, and waterproof connectors your budget allows. Good transmitting antennas are usually good receiving antennas, but the reverse is not always true, so choosing the right VHF antenna and coaxial cable for your particular needs requires expert advice from a reputable supplier. A large sailboat with a masthead antenna may have 100 feet (30 m) between the radio and antenna. Choosing the correct cable is essential for limiting losses in the system. This is not much of a problem in a powerboat.

With a transmitter that has an output of 25 W, you should aim to radiate as much as possible from the antenna. Place the an-

Tip If you intend to carry an emergency antenna in case the primary antenna is damaged, make sure that you can easily get to the antenna socket at the back of the radio.

tenna as high as you can to get the best line of sight, which, on a sailing vessel, is usually at the top of the main mast. If you site it lower down, it will most likely foul the sails and running rigging, and you will probably discover that other structures obscure radio signals on particular courses. Powerboats generally use whip antennas (a self-supporting, flexible antenna, usually sheathed in fiberglass) that must be mounted in the upright position for maximum radiation.

The antenna and its coaxial cable are the most critical parts of the system and the easiest to damage. They require routine care and inspection. All antennas should be kept clean, salt deposits removed, and any brackets and cables checked for damage. Before doing any maintenance work on the antenna, ensure that the power source is disconnected from the equipment and that the main fuses are removed and kept in a safe place.

Tip Antennas are designed to work in the upright position, so don't rake the antenna back to blend in with the flying bridge. It will lose up to 40 percent of its effective coverage area.

Radio Signal

All VHF radio waves, whether sent by digital or analog means, travel in straight lines from their source, but the distance at which they can be received is determined by the earth's curvature. This is why VHF radio is often described as a "line-of-sight" form of radio propagation. Consequently, it follows that the higher the antenna, the farther over the horizon a radio

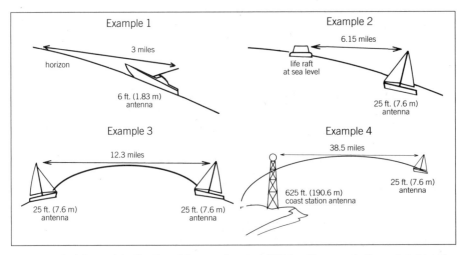

Antenna Height and Radio Signal Range. Because VHF radio range is line-of-sight only, the actual range of your radio will depend on the heights of the transmitting and receiving antennas, as well as on atmospheric conditions that might interfere with or enhance range. See the accompanying text for explanations of the examples.

wave can travel. Here is a rough guide to the distance a radio signal can travel without being lost in the atmosphere:

- boat-to-boat communications, 10–15 miles
- boat-to-shore, 25 miles

If you wish to be somewhat more precise and calculate the approximate distance to the radio horizon of your or any other antenna, apply the following formula. There are several formulas in use, but they all yield roughly the same answer.

distance in nautical miles = 1.23 $\sqrt{\text{height of the antenna in feet}}$
(or 2.25 $\sqrt{\text{height of the antenna in meters}}$)

Don't worry, the math is relatively easy, as you can see from the following examples.

Example 1

You are in the cockpit of a small boat or standing in a life raft. The antenna height of your handheld radio is only likely to be about 6 feet (1.83 m) above sea level, so the math for your radio range will look like this:

distance in nautical miles = 1.23 $\sqrt{6}$

= 1.23 × 2.45

= 3 miles

Not far, is it!

Example 2

You are in a boat with an antenna height of 25 feet (7.6 m), speaking to someone at sea level, sitting in a life raft. Your radio range will therefore be about 6 miles.

distance in nautical miles = 1.23 $\sqrt{25}$

= 1.23 × 5

= 6.15 miles

Example 3

You are speaking to another boat with the same antenna height—25 feet (7.6 m)—as the antenna on your own boat.

Your radio horizon is 6.15 miles (see example 2) and so is the other boat's, so your total radio range is 12.3 miles.

Example 4
Your antenna height is 25 feet (7.6 m), and you're speaking to a coast station whose antenna is 625 feet (190.6 m) above sea level. Their radio horizon is

distance in nautical miles = $1.23 \sqrt{625}$

= 1.23 × 25

= 30.75 miles

Add 30.75 miles to your radio horizon of 6.15 miles (see example 2), and the total is around 37 miles.

If you can't be bothered to get out the calculator, use the accompanying table. VHF radio waves can be affected by atmospheric conditions that often give greater ranges than normal. This is known as *ducting*. There are parts of the U.S. coast, southern regions in particular, where relatively long-distance VHF communications are almost routine. In the Gulf of Mexico, using a 6-foot (1.8 m) mobile antenna and an antenna on a 500-foot (152.5 m) tower, distances of 59 miles have been regularly documented over an extensive test period. In this situation, using this table you would expect a radio horizon of only 30 miles!

➤ **Antenna Heights and Theoretical Radio Horizons**

Antenna Height, ft. (m)	Radio Horizon, nautical miles	Antenna Height, ft. (m)	Radio Horizon, nautical miles
5 (1.5)	2.75	45 (13.7)	8.25
10 (3.1)	3.90	50 (15.3)	8.70
15 (4.6)	4.75	55 (16.8)	9.10
20 (6.1)	5.50	60 (18.3)	9.50
25 (7.6)	6.15	65 (19.8)	9.90
30 (9.2)	6.75	70 (21.4)	10.30
35 (10.7)	7.30	75 (22.9)	10.65
40 (12.2)	7.80	80 (24.4)	11.00

All distances are calculated for average signal strength in average weather conditions and average atmospheric pressure and therefore should be used only as a rough guide.

Within the theoretical radio horizon, digital signals are generally more efficient than voice signals are, and in most cases will extend farther than voice signals, sometimes by as much as 20 percent. Voice signals can often fade away to the extent that they cannot be understood before they reach their theoretical radio horizon. Both high and low power levels on the radio will give the signal sufficient power to reach the limit of the radio horizon, but high power will overcome any losses in the system caused by an imperfect installation. However, this ability of digital signals to be deciphered at a greater distance than voice signals is both the good and the bad news of the new system.

The good news is that the digital signal will almost always get through, provided the radio is able to transmit the signal. The bad news is that when you change to voice communications the signal may fade before it reaches the digital signal horizon. This weakness means that if you are transmitting on the outer fringes of the digital radio horizon, the coast guard will receive your distress alert and therefore know your position and identity, but may not be able to hear the follow-up distress message by voice on CH16. This is one of the reasons it's so important to ensure that the position in the alert is correct.

In this situation, you may have to rely on another vessel's hearing your distress message on CH16 and relaying it to the coast guard on your behalf. In the future, fewer vessels and coast stations will maintain a listening watch on CH16 in favor of conducting all communication by DSC. Sometime in the future, *compulsory ships* (those compelled to conform to GMDSS regulations) may be allowed to drop the CH16 watch altogether. It's expected that other coast stations, such as those formerly manned by marine operators—for example, a coast radio station or a port operations station—will quickly follow suit.

Emergency Antennas

Sailing vessels will probably carry their VHF antennas at the masthead. Consequently, if the vessel is dismasted, the crew will lose the means to call for help. Damage to the radio antenna is not limited to sailing vessels, so it's important for all vessels to carry an emergency antenna that can be fitted quickly to the vessel and the back of the radio.

There is evidence that vessels should consider carrying a handheld VHF radio, with its own battery and antenna, as an emergency backup to the primary radio and for use in a life raft (see chapter 3). In emergencies, the ship's battery is often among the first casualties, and without it the fixed radio will not work. If you do carry a portable VHF as an emergency radio, remember that the reduced antenna height and limited power don't have the same radio horizon as the fixed unit.

Testing the Radio

Voice Channels: A responsible skipper should always check that the VHF radio is working before the vessel sets out to sea. If you request a "radio check" you are actually asking, "What is the strength and clarity of my transmission?" As there is no way to measure a signal on a marine VHF radio, most people reply that they are receiving you "loud and clear."

Calling on CH16 for a radio check is generally frowned upon. Check your radio by hailing another vessel on CH09, or your marina control on its working channel. If you get a reply, the radio is working.

Digital Selective Calling Controller: A DSC radio may be able to test itself without emitting a signal. Check under "Other" in the Safety and Calling menu, and follow the manufacturer's instructions in your radio handbook. *Under no circumstances should you test the controller by transmitting a live distress alert.* It's also not permitted to make a call on CH70 to test the DSC controller.

> **WARNING:** Severe fines may be applied to vessel owners who make false alerts—intentional or not—or who repeatedly make inadvertent false distress calls without canceling them in accordance with the proper procedures (see chapter 11).

CHAPTER 6

Setting Up the DSC-Equipped Radio

Once the radio is installed, don't delay in familiarizing yourself with the radio's capabilities. Run through the various functions and understand exactly what each button does, using this book in conjunction with your operator's handbook.

Check out the CH16 dedicated button. Does the power level automatically change to high power? If not, make a note of this and post it by the radio to remind yourself. Transmitting a distress message on low rather than high power may make the difference between your call being heard and not being heard.

Check out any lighting options of the display and buttons. Can they be dimmed to preserve night sight? Is it a one- or two-handed task?

In chapter 4 we introduced the DSC controller, which is basically the brains and the display of the DSC unit. There are several ways to customize the DSC controller to suit your own boating needs. All these setup functions are found under "Other" or a similar title in the DSC menu and they allow you to

- store an MMSI in the directory
- enter a manual position and time if your radio is not permanently connected to a GPS or loran
- enter a group MMSI number (see page ■■■)
- test the DSC unit using the self-test feature, which tests the internal functions of the radio without transmitting a signal

Programming the Directory

Select "Other" from your DSC menu.

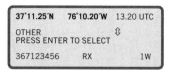

1. Select "Store Directory Calls."
2. Scroll to the next available "Directory Number."
3. Use the numeric keypad to enter the MMSI number and (if your radio allows) type in any explanatory text.
4. Press ENTER to store it.

Tip If your radio doesn't have a directory-naming feature, note the station name and its MMSI in the ship's log or other convenient place for reference.

Setting Manual Position and Time

1. Select "Position."
2. Use the numeric keypad to enter current latitude position.
3. Use the SCROLL button to change from N to S.
4. Use the numeric keypad to enter current longitude.
5. Use the SCROLL button to change from E to W.
6. Use the numeric keypad to enter the time (UTC).
7. Press ENTER to confirm.

Tip For boaters in the United States, in directory memory location 1 store the group MMSI number of the U.S. Coast Guard (003669999; see pages 137–39 for more on group MMSI numbers); and in memory location 2 store the MMSI number of your local coast guard (e.g., 003669933 for Hampton Roads, Virginia; see list in appendix 6).

If the position and time are not updated within 23 ½ hours, the position will default to a series of 9s and the time to a series of 8s.

Entering a Group MMSI Number

Boat clubs, flotillas, regattas, and other nautical organizations may use a group MMSI number for communications. This eliminates the need to call a selected group of vessels individually and is one of the assets of using DSC.

The group number is decided by using one of the MMSIs of the group, dropping the last number and inserting a zero at the beginning. Thus, MMSI number 367123456 would become 036712345. Each member of the group must program the number into the DSC unit. Once programmed, each radio will respond to both its individual MMSI number and the group MMSI number. It's a good idea to store the number in the directory ready for immediate use. A group MMSI number cannot be used as a single vessel's identity.

To program a group MMSI number:

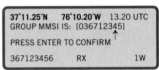

1. Select "Enter Group MMSI?"
2. Use the numeric keypad to enter the MMSI number.
3. Press ENTER to confirm.

Self-Test Feature (if Fitted)

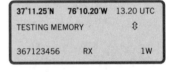

1. Select "Self Test?"
2. Each individual function test will be displayed in turn.
3. Unless a fault is detected, an alarm will sound and "Self Test Completed" will be displayed.

Once you have completed customizing your DSC controller, select CANCEL/CLEAR to return to the radio function.

CHAPTER 7

The Batteries

Marine radios, like many other pieces of boat equipment, require batteries in order to work. Some portable equipment (handheld VHF radio, EPIRBs, etc.) only requires small, internal 1.5- to 10-volt cells. Other larger units, such as an installed VHF radio, require both connection to the ship's high-ampere storage battery and small internal batteries to retain the unit's memory functions, such as MMSI numbers in a directory. Given their importance, a little knowledge about battery care and maintenance is vital.

Small, Internal Batteries

Most of these cells cannot be recharged. The main areas of use are in search-and-rescue transponders (SARTs), emergency position-indicating radio beacons (EPIRBs), lights on lifebuoys and danbuoys, and flashlights. Many electronic instruments, including the VHF radio, rely on a such batteries to preserve the unit's internal memory. Check these batteries regularly for expiration dates and their state of charge, and immediately replace any doubtful ones with the type specified by the equipment manufacturer. To facilitate this, keep a log that itemizes equipment that uses these batteries, note the battery's exact specification, and note the date it was last checked.

Ship's Battery

Ship's batteries are rechargeable and generally referred to as 12-volt *storage* or *service* batteries. The main battery or batteries used aboard the vessel powers electrical and electronic equipment ranging from a refrigerator to a VHF radio. It is recharged from the vessel's engine, a separate generator, or a battery charger connected to the utility company's power system. It's usually housed in the bilge, where the weight is useful in keeping the center of gravity low. Unfortunately, this makes it vulnerable if the boat floods or catches fire, and with the battery out of action the radio won't work, either. You could consider fitting a dedicated battery for the radio in a place that affords greater protection.

The ship's batteries come in three basic types:

- lead acid
- gel or sealed batteries
- nickel-cadmium

Because lead-acid batteries use sulfuric acid as the electrolyte, you can see the battery's state of charge by measuring its specific gravity with a hydrometer. A fully charged battery has a specific gravity of between 1,260 and 1,290, and a discharged battery will be about 1,160. If you use a hydrometer with color coding, use the following rule: if the float is in the green, the battery is OK; if it's in the red, it needs to be topped with distilled water.

The only way you can determine the state of charge of a gel or sealed battery is to measure its terminal voltage. Fully charged, it should read 12.6 volts. There is no way to top up these batteries, so once the plates inside begin to gas or dry out, the battery is doomed.

Nickel-cadmium batteries are virtually indestructible and most have a life span of up to 25 years, but their drawbacks are expense and bulk.

Battery Care

A battery must be correctly connected into the electrical circuit, that is, the positive battery terminal must be connected to the positive connection and likewise with the negative terminal. Connecting the wrong way around has the potential to damage both the battery and the equipment.

Here's how to care for your lead acid, gel, and nickel-cadmium batteries.

Tip If the terminals on your ship's batteries are not well marked, improve their marking yourself with a large clear (+) for the positive terminal and a (–) for the negative. This could save you an expensive lesson.

- Batteries are heavy, so ensure that your battery bank is adequately secured. In the event of a knockdown, you don't want the battery to get loose and punch a hole in the side of the vessel, or become a missile lethal to the crew.
- House the battery in a purpose-designed battery box that will allow the flammable hydrogen gas to escape but not allow seawater in.
- During the charging cycle, when hydrogen gas is given off, ventilate the area well and don't smoke close by.
- Regularly check the electrolyte level and top up to ¼ inch (0.6 cm) above the plates with *distilled* water as required.
- Battery acid is corrosive, so wear gloves and old clothing when working on the battery.
- Try to fit vents that won't allow battery acid to pour out if the boat gets caught out in a rough sea.
- On a routine basis, check for signs of corrosion and ensure that the top of the battery is kept clean. This will prevent stray currents flowing between the terminals and discharging the battery.
- Smear a layer of petroleum jelly over the terminals to protect them from corrosion.

- Some rechargeable batteries that power handheld radios, cellular phones, laptop computers, and so forth must be discharged completely before recharging. In older nickel-cadmium batteries, this will prevent their developing a "memory" that limits their charging capacity. Newer nickel-metalhydride batteries do not develop memories.
- If you carry a handheld VHF, ensure that you always have a fully charged spare battery on board, perhaps kept in the "abandon-ship bag," or "grab-bag." If possible, buy equipment

> **WARNING:** Remember that the radio relies on a vessel's service battery that relies on an alternator that relies on an engine that relies on clean fuel, clean water, and regular maintenance. Ignore any part of the system at your peril!

that can accept alkaline cells, which can be kept on board for extended periods and will be fully charged when needed.

CHAPTER 8

VHF Marine Radio Channels

Channel Numbering

The ITU has allocated to the Maritime Mobile Service VHF frequencies between 156.00 and 163.00 MHz, which are already converted into preprogrammed, numbered channels when you purchase your radio. You cannot dial in individual frequencies.

These numbered channels make up the International Maritime VHF Bandplan (see appendix 3), which is in use worldwide. However, the United States and Canada have been allowed to use these frequencies in such a way so radios designed for use in either country come with a choice of preprogrammed options. For example channels 02, 04, and 60 are not available in U.S. radios. They are reserved for use in Canada by the Canadian Coast Guard. When you buy a radio in either the United States or Canada, it should come to you with the appropriate channel-numbering system already specified. If it doesn't, there should be a switch or menu option that allows you to toggle between the U.S. and international channel-numbering systems.

Outside U.S. waters, you must switch to the international system. Complete lists of the U.S., Canadian, and international maritime channels are given in appendices 1, 2, and 3.

Single- and Dual-Frequency Channels and Half-Duplex Communications

As seen in the accompanying excerpt from the U.S. Maritime Bandplan, on some channels, such as CH22A, ships transmit and receive on the same frequency, in this case 157.100 MHz—these are *single-frequency channels*.

➤ Maritime Channels (Excerpt)

Channel Number	Ship Transmit, MHz	Ship Receive, MHz	Use
22A	157.100	157.100	Coast guard liaison and maritime safety information broadcasts. Broadcasts announced on CH16
23A	157.150	157.150	U.S. Coast Guard only
24	157.200	161.800	Public correspondence (Marine operator)

Source: *U.S. Maritime Bandplan, ITU.*

Other channels, such as CH24, use different frequencies for transmitting and receiving, in this case 157.200 MHz (transmit) and 161.800 MHz (receive). These are *dual-frequency channels*.

Because VHF radios come preprogrammed, these differences might seem academic, but they can have an impact on what we hear.

Single-Frequency Channels

Geek-Speak

Single-frequency channels (e.g., 22A and 72) are also known as "simplex" channels.

Single-frequency (simplex) channels use the *same frequency* for transmitting and receiving. The transmit button (also called the press-to-transmit, or PTT button) on the microphone toggles between these two functions—press to transmit, release to receive. A third party listening in can hear both sides of a conversation if both transmitters are within range, because the third radio is receiving both signals.

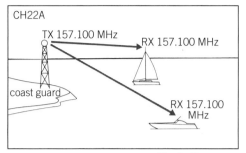 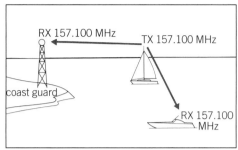

Single-Frequency Communications

Dual-Frequency Channels

If you're already familiar with VHF radios, you may have wondered why, when listening in on certain radio conversations, particularly those to telephone subscribers ashore, you can only hear the shore-side part of the conversation. The reason is that dual-frequency channels are in use. These channels use two frequencies, one to transmit a signal and the second to receive a signal.

> **WARNING:** Whenever you use a marine VHF radio on a simplex channel, be aware that your conversation can be overheard by any other station within radio range whose radio is tuned to the channels you are using.

An example is CH24, a public correspondence channel. This has a ship transmitting frequency of 157.200 MHz and a receiving frequency of 161.800 MHz. The coast station will receive on 157.200 and transmit on 161.800. To utilize this feature fully requires a radio that can receive and transmit simultaneously so that a normal two-way conversation can be held. For this purpose, two independent antennas are needed, one for receiving and one for transmitting; they are usually found only on larger vessels.

> **Geek-Speak**
>
> Dual-frequency channels are also known as "duplex" channels.

Vessels fitted with a duplex radio will continue to hear only the coast station side of the conversation because the radio is not set up to receive on the ship-transmit frequency. In 1997, international radio regulations were modified to permit several dual-frequency channels in the International Bandplan to be split into two same-frequency channels to meet increasing needs for simplex VHF channels. Check with your service provider or with the coast guard to see which channels, if any, have been changed in your area. This is the case in several U.S. and Canadian channels, including CH22. The designation for such single-frequency send-and-receive channels is "A."

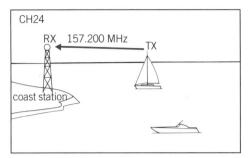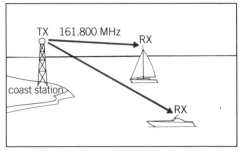

Half-Duplex Communications

Half-Duplex Communication

VHF and VHF-DSC radios on most recreational vessels use both single- and dual-frequency channels but can only use dual-frequency channels in the way described as "half-duplex." A half-duplex radio uses one antenna that switches between the two frequencies in turn. When you want to transmit on a dual-frequency channel, push the transmit switch and the radio tunes automatically to the ship-transmit frequency; when you want an answer, release the switch and the radio retunes automatically to the ship-receive frequency. Consequently, you cannot have a simultaneous two-way conversation.

Tip The letter A after a channel number indicates the single-frequency use of a channel used in other parts of the world as a dual-frequency channel. Local operations are different from international operations on that channel. "A" channels are generally only used in the United States and Canada, and their use is normally not recognized or allowed outside these waters. If you take your boat abroad, you'll need to switch to the International Maritime VHF Bandplan (see appendix 3).

For example, in the accompanying illustration, the sailboat transmits a message to the coast station at 157.200 MHz; the coast station receives the message on that frequency but responds on 161.800 MHz, which is received by both the sailboat and the powerboat. Because the powerboat is in receive mode of CH24, it will not hear the transmission from the sailboat.

The only duplex channels a boater is likely to use are those for making telephone calls linked to the land-based phone system. It's wise to warn any likely recipients of such phone calls that the conversation will be stilted and that the person will need to say "Over" to cue you to speak, and vice versa.

Capture Effect

When you aren't transmitting, the radio will lock onto the strongest signal it receives that breaks the squelch level set on the tuned channel. Known as the *capture effect*, this is the reason for two power levels (high and low) on every VHF radio. You should therefore only use the lowest power that will allow communication to take place, unless your call demands high power as in the case of distress communications. To understand why, imagine

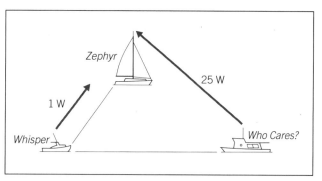

The Capture Effect

two vessels, *Whisper* and *Zephyr*, which are 1 mile apart and communicating on low power. Another vessel, *Who Cares?*, which is 2 miles away, tunes to the same channel and begins transmitting using high power. *Who Cares?'*s transmission on high power, though farther away, will overwhelm the signal from *Whisper*'s and *Zephyr*'s low-power transmissions, and this will be experienced as interference. As soon as the vessel on high power ceases transmitting, the receiving station will again receive low-power transmissions. Transmitting on high power can unnecessarily annoy other vessels: if you try transmitting on low power but get no response, then you may switch to high power, but monitor the channel first to ensure no one else is using it.

When high power is selected, the vessel with the least losses in the radio transmitting system will win the capture-effect war. A poor-quality antenna, unsuitable coaxial cable, or a shoddy radio installation will greatly reduce the radiated power, so although the radio is switched to 25 W, it is rarely the case that 25 W is radiated from the antenna.

GMDSS VHF Channel Usage

The introduction of GMDSS has brought about changes in the way several channels are used:

Channel 06. This is the primary intership channel, but it is also used for communication between ships and aircraft for coordinated search-and-rescue (SAR) operations. For safety reasons, aircraft may also use it to communicate with vessels.

Channel 13. Used for ship-to-ship communication relating to the safety of navigation (e.g., bridge-to-bridge safety). Vessels over 65 feet, 7 inches (20 m) in length must monitor this channel within U.S. waters extending 12 miles offshore. The authorities may fine anyone using this channel improperly. (See also chapter 10.)

Channel 16. Used for voice communications for distress, urgency, and safety traffic (radio communication). Aircraft may also use it for safety purposes. In the past, CH16 was also the general calling (hail) channel to other vessels, but under GMDSS regulations the use of CH16 should be limited to distress, urgency, and safety traffic only. In vessels that don't have DSC, CH16 should be used for distress calls, calling ships, or calling the coast guard. Though authorized by the FCC but not monitored by the coast guard, CH09 has been allocated as the alternative calling channel for boaters and is also the preferred channel for general-purpose calls between ships and to coast stations. (For further information on CH09, see page 47.) In Canadian waters, vessels still need to use CH16 for making an initial call to other vessels and the coast guard.

Channel 70. Allows only digital selective calling for distress (see chapters 10 and 11), urgency, safety alerting, and routine calling where you cannot directly use a working channel. You will need to know the MMSI number of the station you wish to call, except in the case of a distress or "All Ships" call (see chapter 4).

PART 2

VHF RADIO
PROTOCOL

CHAPTER 9

Standard Procedure

Language Requirement

Thankfully, the English language is internationally recognized for radiotelephony use. Had Marconi taken his discovery to China or Spain, we English-speakers could have been in trouble. So put yourself in the shoes of those whose first language *isn't* English, and imagine what a nightmare communicating over the radio must be. This is why we need to use a standard procedure.

Standard procedure provides a familiar pattern, understood by radio operators across the globe. When standard phrases or words are used in a predetermined order, they're much easier to discern, particularly where there is background interference or poor accents. A departure from the standard procedure often creates confusion that reduces the reliability and speed of communication.

Tip Though maritime radio exists for professional and recreational mariners alike, it's important to communicate like a professional and to learn the procedure.

Position, Course, Distance, and Speed

To improve understanding, the following pieces of information are always given in order: position, then course, then distance, then speed.

Position

Position can be given by either latitude and longitude or by bearing.

By Latitude and Longitude

By tradition, latitude is always expressed first, longitude second. Each is expressed in degrees, minutes, and tenths of a minute. Latitude must be specified as either N (north of the equator) or S (south of the equator) and longitude as E (east of Greenwich) or W (west of the Greenwich), as in "My position is 37°11.3´ N, 76°10.2´ W." GPS and DSC units represent latitude and longitude this way, as well.

Position by Bearing

Where position is related to a bearing of a charted object, the object should be easy to find and understand. For example, it should be a well-known headland rather than an obscure buoy. The bearing must be given in three-figure notation from true north, and you must make it clear whether the bearing is *to* the charted object, as in a GPS waypoint, or *from* the charted object. For example, "My position is 180 degrees true from Point Reyes," which would be written as "180 deg (T) from Point Reyes."

Course

Your course is the direction in which your boat is heading. Courses are given in three-figure notation from true north. A northeasterly course will be expressed as 045°(T), not 45°(T). For example, "My course is zero four five degrees true," written as "045 deg (T)."

If you read the course directly from a compass, do not forget to apply variation and deviation to get true. When converting a compass course to a true course, easterly variation and deviation are *added* to the bearing, whereas westerly variation and deviation are *subtracted*.

Distance

Distances are expressed in nautical miles and tenths of a mile (cables) except in some inland waters such as the Great Lakes and along the Intracoastal Waterway, where statute miles are used. For example, "My distance is 20.50 miles."

Speed

Speed is usually expressed in knots. One knot equals one nautical mile per hour. Unless otherwise stated, it refers to your speed through the water and is the speed you read from your vessel's log. For example, my speed is "20 knots."

If you mean speed over the ground, as read from your chart or GPS, then this must be stated as "ground speed."

Geographical Names

Place names should be those used on charts with latitude and longitude positions as necessary. For example, "Point Reyes."

Time

Time is expressed using the 24-hour clock, with the indication of whether you are using UTC (previously known as GMT), zone time, or local time. For example, "eighteen hundred hours" (6 P.M.) Eastern Standard Time is also written as "23.00 UTC." See UTC in the glossary for conversion formula.

Phonetic Alphabet

The phonetic alphabet was devised by an international NATO committee to offer the most suitable words for pronunciation by radio operators of different nationalities, languages, and accents. It is recommended by the International Telecommunication Union (ITU) for use in all voice communications where reception is poor or where a word or words can be confusing to spell. Examples are place names such as Whangarei (a port in New Zealand), vessel names, foreign words, words with weak syllables such as "poor" and "paw" and groups of letters within the text of a message, such as a vessel or operator's call sign.

To achieve the standard pronunciation of each word, emphasize the syllables in capital letters.

➤ Phonetic Alphabet

Letter	Word	Pronunciation	Letter	Word	Pronunciation
A	Alfa	*AL-fah*	N	November	*no-VEM-ber*
B	Bravo	*BRAH-voh*	O	Oscar	*OSS-car*
C	Charlie	*CHAR-lee*	P	Papa	*pah-PAH*
D	Delta	*DELL-tah*	Q	Quebec	*keh-BECK*
E	Echo	*ECK-oh*	R	Romeo	*ROW-meoh*
F	Foxtrot	*FOKS-trot*	S	Sierra	*see-AIR-rah*
G	Golf	*golf*	T	Tango	*TAN-go*
H	Hotel	*hoh-TELL*	U	Uniform	*YOU-neeform*
I	India	*IN-deeah*	V	Victor	*VIK-tah*
J	Juliet	*jewlee-ETT*	W	Whiskey	*WISS-key*
K	Kilo	*KEY-loh*	X	X-ray	*ECKS-ray*
L	Lima	*LEE-mah*	Y	Yankee	*YANG-key*
M	Mike	*mike*	Z	Zulu	*ZOO-loo*

Before plunging into the phonetic alphabet, warn the radio operator of the receiving station that you are about to spell the last word or group of words phonetically. You do this by saying the word or phrase you want to spell and follow it with the words "I spell," then spell the word phonetically.

If you have the opportunity to name a vessel, think about how it will sound over the radio and how easy it is to understand. Unusual spellings such as "Xanthippe," "Hoof Hearted," or "Tahiti Douche" may seem truly inspired after a night in the bar, but they will test your phonetic alphabet skills on almost every radio call. A name like "On the Rocks," "That Sinkin' Feelin'," or "Stranded" may cause confusion to a coast guard radio operator, and a simple name like "Hello" when repeated three times, could have you sounding like a London policeman. Also, think about the length of the name. "Invocation to the Great Bear" not only takes on the mantle of a short-story title when repeated three times, but you'll need a lucky streak in Las Vegas to afford a sign writer to paint the name on your boat.

Tip Write the vessel's name phonetically on a card posted in plain sight close to the radio.

The following example of one boat calling another shows how routinely you might wind up spelling your boat name.

Blue Gull, Blue Gull
This is Yulan, Yulan
I spell, yankee, uniform, lima, alfa, november
Channel 78
Over

Phonetic Numerals

When numbers are transmitted, poor pronunciation can confuse the operator at the receiving end. "Five" and "nine" especially can sound alike, so it's important to pronounce them as given in the accompanying table. Send numbers digit by digit, using the pronunciation set out here when conditions are poor (great distance or atmospheric interference):

➤ Spelling and Pronouncing Numbers

Number	Spelling	Pronunciation	Number	Spelling	Pronunciation
0	zero	*ZEE-roe*	5	five	*fife*
1	one	*wun*	6	six	*six*
2	two	*too*	7	seven	*SEV-en*
3	three	*tree*	8	eight	*ait*
4	four	*FOE-wer*	9	nine	*NIGH-ner*

The following example shows how one boat might confirm a marine dock assignment.

Blue Gull, Blue Gull
Berth B59
That is, bravo, fife, nighner
Out

Procedure Words

When you're using a VHF radio, certain familiar English words and phrases make you more easily understood all over the world. They are words like "Roger" and phrases like "Say again." Sometimes known as "standard procedural words" (prowords), they are words that radio operators of all nationalities *expect* to hear and instantly understand when they do.

The International Maritime Organization (IMO) has devoted an entire manual to standard procedural words. The following is a list of the commonly used prowords that a recreational boater is most likely to hear, so try to learn them. They are not listed in any particular order.

➤ Prowords in Common Use

THIS IS	This transmission is from the station whose name or call sign follows.
DELTA ECHO	Used instead of *this is* where there are language difficulties. (The phrase is the phonetic spelling of "de," French for "from.")
OVER	An invitation to reply to your transmission.
OUT	Signifies the end of communications and no reply is expected.
I SPELL	This signifies your intention to spell the last word or group of letters phonetically.
IN LETTERS	The following numeral or group of numerals should be written in letters, as in "Six Forks Road."
IN FIGURES	The following numeral or group of numerals should be written as figures, as in "6 Forks Road."
RECEIVED	Used to acknowledge the receipt of a message.
ROGER	Indicates that you have received and understood the message.
SAY AGAIN	Used when you require a message or part of a message to be repeated or emphasized. Unless you want the whole message repeated, it is used with one of the following phrases to indicate the part of the message to be repeated: ⊙ word after ⊙ word before ⊙ all after ⊙ all before ⊙ all between
I SAY AGAIN	This response to *say again* indicates that you are about to repeat all or part of a message.
I READ BACK	If a receiving station is doubtful about all or part of a message, it may repeat the message to the transmitting station. The station precedes the repetition with "I read back."
CORRECTION	Spoken during the transmission of a message, indicating that an error has been made and is about to be corrected.
WRONG	Used by the receiving station if a message has incorrectly been repeated back.
RADIO CHECK	This means: "Please tell me the strength and clarity of my radio signal." Radio checks are classed as test calls and as such must take no longer than 10 seconds.
STATION CALLING	Used when a station receives a call intended for it, but is uncertain of the identity of the station calling. For example: "Station calling *(your boat's name)* say again your name."

Transmitting Rules: The Radio Creed

Transmitting rules are the radio operator's gospel. They are simple rules, created internationally for the efficient use of radio channels and frequencies. Transgressions will conjure up the winged demons from the U.S. Federal Communications Commission (FCC), which not only will impose on you a hefty fine, and possibly a prison sentence, but they might also pluck out your vital organs to feed to their slavering young! You've been warned.

You must not do any of the following.

⊘ **Transmit false distress, safety, or identification signals.** It is a serious offense to transmit hoax distress calls or any other hoax calls. Regardless of how much you want to ride in a rescue helicopter, it is illegal to call for help when you don't need it. False signals that are malicious carry severe penalties. Be very careful if you have inquisitive, bored, or delinquent kids near a DSC radio with its tempting red button.

> **WARNING:** The U.S. Coast Guard warns that a growing number of boaters, unsuccessful in getting a radio check on VHF CH16, are making Mayday calls to get a response. Every hoax—and that includes Mayday radio checks—is subject to prosecution as a class D felony under Title 14, Section 85, of the U.S. Code. At the time of writing, the penalties are a $5,000 fine plus all costs the coast guard incurs as a result of the perpetrator's action. Since hoaxes can mask genuine distress calls and lead to the loss of life, the U.S. Coast Guard and the FCC are working closely together to detect offending radio operators.

⊘ **Transmit obscene, profane, or indecent language.** If another vessel has ignored the rule of the road and forced you to give way when it should have been the stand-on vessel, you cannot imply over the air that the master's parents weren't married, that the master's mother was a female canine, or that the master resembles any bodily orifice.

⊘ **Broadcast messages or programs without expecting a reply.** The radio is licensed for two-way communication, not broadcasting. Note than an "all ships" call (see chapter 4) is not classed as a broadcast but is a call addressed to all stations monitoring that channel.

⊘ **Close down before finishing all operations resulting from a distress call, urgency, or safety signal.** If you become involved in an emergency situation, lives and the safety of a vessel may depend on your radio link to the coast guard remaining open. Discuss the situation with the coast guard before signing off.

⊘ **Make unnecessary transmissions.** Unnecessary transmissions involve communications not concerned with ship's business.

⊘ **Transmit superfluous signals.** Superfluous signals indicate that your radio or its installation could be faulty. It should be investigated and repaired before making further transmissions. This must be carried out by or under the supervision of an FCC-licensed technician if your vessel is registered in the United States.

⊘ **Operate a VHF radio without the authority of the master of the vessel.** Permission to use the radio must be given by the master of the vessel before any calls may be made.

⊘ **Broadcast messages intended for reception at addresses on shore.** An example would be an operator of a fishing vessel who has a radio scanner at home to monitor the whereabouts of the boat. The fisherman cannot broadcast any message to a receiver at home.

⊘ **Broadcast or transmit music.** You can't liven up the boater's channel with a sea shanty or a Sunday morning gospel sing-along.

⊘ **Transmit messages intended for reception at addresses on shore, except through a coast radio station.** It is forbidden to use a marine VHF radio in place of a normal telephone unless you have the capability to direct-dial into the land-based phone network. You can use Citizen's Band radio, a cellular phone, or, if you are a licensed radio amateur, ham radio.

⊘ **Use your first (given) name, or other names, in lieu of the ship's name or call sign.** So, if your friend's given name is George and he calls you The Smoking Gun, you cannot say "Hey, George, it's the Smoking Gun—come back" or other Citizen's Band talk.

⊘ **Transmit without identifying the ship station.** A ship station identity can be the vessel's name, its call sign, or its nine-digit Maritime Mobile Service Identity (MMSI) number (see page 17). For recreational craft, it is usually the vessel's name.

⊘ **Use frequencies other than those permitted by the U.S. or Canadian Governments for VHF marine radio use.** When boating abroad, the International Maritime VHF Band applies (see appendix 3).

⊘ **Divulge the contents of a radio message.** The ITU Radio Regulations require the responsible radio operator, licensed or unlicensed, and any other person aboard who has knowledge of any radio communications not to divulge the contents or even the existence of any correspondence that is transmitted, intercepted, or received.

Microphone Skills

Your first attempt to use a radio can be daunting, particularly if you're speaking to a radio professional. Pressing the PTT switch for the first time, I felt as if I were taking to the stage and giving my first public performance. Don't worry; a little practice, some call planning, a deep breath, and the recommendations below will soon help you to relax.

The requirement for clear speech over the radio is obvious, since a message that is difficult to understand is about as useful as a naval officer on the foredeck. There are several factors to bear in mind:

Voice. Pitch it at a slightly higher level than for normal conversation. Try to avoid the tendency to drop the pitch of the voice at the end of a word or phrase, otherwise words are likely to be lost.

Clarity. Speak clearly and emphasize weak syllables in order that a word such as *poor* is not mistaken for *paw*. Operators with strong regional or national accents must make a special effort, particularly if English is not their first language.

Volume. The microphone should be held 2 to 3 inches (5–8 cm) in front of, and slightly to the side of, the mouth. Speak at normal conversation level and avoid shouting, which may overload the microphone and cause distortion and damage. If people receiving your calls cannot hear you properly, tell them to use the volume control.

Speed. Messages to be written down should be sent slowly and in normal phrases rather than word by word. We're used to hearing language in this way, whereas words individually spoken have you guessing at what comes next and sound disjointed. Pause at the end of each phrase to allow time for the words to be written down, and keep in mind that the average speeds per minute for reading, speaking, and writing words are 250, 150, and 20, respectively.

Tip To sound confident, write down beforehand exactly what you intend to say.

CHAPTER 10

Calling Etiquette

Calling Channels

Channel 70

Channel 70 is assigned for digital selective calling (DSC) for distress, urgency, safety, and routine calls to other ships and services. DSC radios are designed so that only DSC can be used on CH70, and while CH70 can be accessed manually, no voice communications can take place. Unless the radio is fitted with two antennas, nothing is likely to be received when the radio is transmitting. All DSC radios keep their own watch on CH70 automatically. You don't need to physically listen to CH70. You can monitor another channel such as CH16 while the radio itself listens to CH70 automatically.

Channel 70 can cope with up to 500 routine calls an hour. Once a call is acknowledged, the system automatically switches the radio to the appropriate working channel, and clears CH70 for the next DSC call. A distress alert is different: five consecutive calls are transmitted one after the other to ensure that the alert gets through. If the first one or two coincide with other DSC traffic, the remaining three will make it through, and it only requires one of the five to be successful.

Some single-receiver radios are able to scan CH70 and nondigital channels. Check the specification of your radio in your owner's manual to decide whether this scan feature is likely to be effective in detecting signals on CH70 and other analog voice channels.

When an alert is received on CH70, an alarm sounds. The alarm for a distress or urgency alert is different from that of a safety or routine alert. However, be aware that many pieces of modern electronic equipment have alarms and, unfortunately, many of them sound alike. Try to get to know your radio alarms and, if at all possible, try to buy equipment that has different-sounding alarms from those already fitted in your vessel.

WARNING: Any alert call—distress or otherwise—made on CH70 is just that: an alert. It must be followed by voice communications on the appropriate working channel.

Channel 16

The use of CH16 is limited to distress, urgency, and safety communications and as a calling channel where DSC cannot be used. To relieve congestion on CH16 and comply with the needs of GMDSS, the U.S. Federal Communications Commission (FCC) has established VHF CH09 as a supplementary intership calling channel for U.S. recreational boaters (see CH09 below). Vessels in Canadian waters must continue to use CH16 to call other ships. Calls to both the U.S. and Canadian Coast Guards also must be made on CH16. Once the coast guards have established VHF-DSC services around the coast, CH70 may be used in preference.

The use of CH16 falls loosely into one of two categories:

- **Distress, urgency, and safety traffic by voice.** Once the initial distress, urgency, or safety alert has been transmitted on CH70, the radio will automatically retune to CH16 for the subsequent voice communication with the acknowledging station.
- **The calling channel.** For U.S. vessels that do not have a DSC radio, or where a vessel's MMSI number is unknown, CH16 is used as a

hailing channel for intership calls prior to changing to a working channel. When calling a recreational vessel, try whenever possible to use CH09, the channel assigned for this purpose. Vessels equipped with a DSC radio will use CH70 for calling, provided that the receiving station's MMSI number is known. Some organizations can be called by voice only on their working channels. In Canadian waters, CH16 is used for calling recreational craft where DSC cannot be used.

The continued use of CH16 as a calling channel by vessels not equipped with DSC is likely to prevent essential distress, urgency, or safety traffic from being broadcast. To keep CH16 free for this essential traffic, all other transmissions on CH16 must not exceed one minute. On the other hand, the time taken to make a digital call on CH70 is virtually instantaneous and this efficiency highlights one of the fundamental differences between CH70 and CH16.

When the DSC controller selects CH16 for distress, urgency, or safety traffic, or when you use the CH16 dedicated button, the radio should select high power automatically, but check your radio to see that it does. With radios that don't automatically select high power, post a notice near the radio to that effect—it may save your life. If you wish to make a call on CH16 where high power is not required, select low power.

When using "Dual Watch" (see page 8) to monitor CH16 and an alternative channel, if a signal is detected on CH16 the receiver will lock onto CH16 for the duration of the transmission. Where a signal is detected on the second channel, the radio will regularly switch back to CH16 for a fraction of a second and briefly interrupt reception on the second channel. If a signal is subsequently detected on CH16, the receiver will remain locked onto it.

Channel 09

Though the U.S. Coast Guard doesn't monitor CH09, the FCC has assigned it as a supplementary calling channel to CH16 for recreational boaters in the United States. This is to relieve congestion on CH16 and comply with the needs of the GMDSS. However, CH09 may cease to be an alternative calling channel, when commercial shipping ceases monitoring CH16. It is permitted to pass short messages on CH09, which is not allowed on CH16. If you do relay a message on CH09, make sure that you do keep it short; otherwise, you'll inconvenience other boaters waiting to use the channel.

Tip To keep CH16 and CH09 free for other traffic and avoid the risk of losing contact with the other station during channel switching, arrange to call other recreational vessels at a prearranged time directly on an agreed working channel.

Channel 13

The GMDSS has been allocated CH13 for bridge-to-bridge safety, and commercial ships are required to maintain a constant watch on this frequency when operating in confined waters. Common sense dictates that other vessels interacting with shipping, particularly in and around busy commercial ports, should do the same by using the "Dual Watch" or "Scan" feature. Messages must only be about ship navigation. They should be kept short and the power level must be kept to 1 W (low power).

Initial Calls

DSC Calls

If you want to use DSC, you must know the MMSI number of the station you wish to call. Just as you must know the subscriber's number before you can make a telephone call on land, you must know the MMSI number of another vessel you wish to call directly on DSC.

Using the handbook supplied with your VHF-DSC radio, either select the other station's MMSI number from the preprogrammed directory, or manually program the MMSI number yourself (see page 27; see also appendix 6 for U.S. and Canadian Coast Guard MMSI numbers). If your radio has a display screen, follow the menu options.

When you're calling a coast station, the coast station chooses the working channel for the reply, and your radio will automatically switch to that channel once your call has been acknowledged. Generally speaking, this is CH16 for distress, urgency, and safety calls, and a working channel (e.g., CH68) for routine calls. When you're calling another vessel, you must choose the working channel for the subsequent voice communications. Some radios may suggest a working channel for you.

Finally, to prevent interference to other stations, ensure the radio is set to the correct power level. For communications with the coast guard or a coast radio station, select high power. For intership and short-range calls to lockkeepers, marinas, bridge attendants, and so forth, select low power. If communications on low power are poor, switch to high power.

The display when you're making a DSC call will look something like this:

Use the ENTER button to send the DSC call.

```
37°11.3'N       76°10.2'W      09.36 UTC
CHANNEL?   68                       ⇕
PRESS ENTER TO SEND
REPLY    CH68
367123456          RX             1W
```

Non-DSC Calls

For calls to a vessel that doesn't have a DSC radio, or a vessel for which you don't know the MMSI number, you must make a voice call. All initial voice calls follow the same six-step procedure:

1. Before making the call, select the correct channel (CH16 or CH09, or another working channel, e.g., CH68, see below) and power level.
2. Check that the channel is clear.
3. Know the identity of the station to be called. This is usually the vessel's name. Where two vessels have the same name, use the

vessel's call sign if you know it. Repeat the identity between one and three times depending on the following points:

- You are calling on a working channel and the station is expecting a call. The radio operator will instantly recognize her vessel's name, so only *one* call is needed.
- The vessel is likely to be monitoring the channel, but not be expecting a call. Repeat the name *twice*, once as an alert, and again to confirm that the call is for that vessel.
- You're involved with distress, urgency, or safety traffic or radio conditions are difficult. Repeat the name *three times*.

4. The words "This is" followed by . . .
5. The name of your station. This is usually the vessel's name or call sign. Use the same number of repetitions you used to identify the called station.
6. "Over."

Once contact is established, identify yourself once on each "Over."

Who Chooses the Working Channel?

Intership

Before the introduction of DSC, the called vessel chose the intership working channel. This stretches back to the early days of VHF on boats when radios were very basic and often came with only two channels: CH16 and the primary intership channel, CH06. That meant you could never be sure that the called station was capable of tuning to more than one working channel. It is still the case with some older portable radios that they have fewer channels available, so the rule is still valid. To save time on CH16 or CH09, and avoid the risk of losing each other during the search for a free channel, the calling station can suggest a working channel that is known to be free. If the called station cannot comply, then the called operator may still choose his own working channel.

When using DSC, the calling vessel chooses the intership working channel. Once the other vessel has acknowledged the call, each radio will automatically retune to the selected channel.

> **Tip** When you call another vessel on CH16 or CH09, suggest a working channel immediately. It saves time yet still allows the called station to nominate an alternative channel.

Ship to Shore

When you're calling a coast station by voice or DSC, the coast station selects the working channel because coast stations are only licensed to use certain channels. Once the coast station has acknowledged the call, your DSC controller will automatically tune to the working channel indicated.

Watchkeeping

Why There Are Rules for Listening

The U.S. Coast Guard cites an example of a charter boat whose radio was not tuned to the proper channel and missed a severe storm warning. By the time the captain learned of the storm, it was too late to return to shore. The vessel sank and several people died. Also, a yacht in trouble off the west coast of Mexico and far from help saw a passenger ship. What could have been a quick rescue nearly turned into a disaster because the passenger ship had its radio switched off and did not receive the yacht's distress call. The yacht was able to attract the ship's attention using flares, and was rescued. And don't forget the *Titanic* disaster. Had radio watchkeeping been mandatory, it's possible that most of the passengers would have been saved and *Titanic*'s only historical note would have been that she sank on her maiden voyage.

There are three VHF marine channels recognized worldwide for safety purposes:

- channel 70 (DSC only)
- channel 16
- channel 13

In the United States, the FCC has also assigned CH09 to boaters as a supplementary calling channel.

In a VHF-DSC radio with two receivers, one continually monitors CH70 and the other monitors a channel of your choice, ideally CH16. It must be remembered that with only one antenna, watchkeeping on CH70 stops when the radio is transmitting. With Dual Watch selected (see page 8), you can monitor a second voice channel. In coastal waters, the U.S. Coast Guard recommends monitoring CH09 as the second channel. If your radio does not have two receivers but is engineered to scan among CH70 and one or two voice channels, such as the case in the SC 101, the radio can only handle one channel at a time: when it is busy on one channel, it will not get signal from the others.

ITU and FCC regulations require boaters with VHF radios to maintain a continuous watch on CH70 (if fitted with a DSC radio) and CH16 whenever the vessel is at sea, the radio is switched on, and the vessel is not communicating with another station. Monitoring CH70 is done automatically by the radio; listening to voice channels is done by the operator. If you monitor CH16 and CH09 in "Dual Watch" mode, the radio will switch between the two channels until a signal is detected on one of them. If a signal is detected on CH09, the radio will switch to CH09 but continue to sample CH16.

When a vessel receives a DSC alert, an alarm sounds and details are displayed on the screen. Once the receiving operator has accepted the call, the radio will automatically switch to the working channel. The minimum radio specification (SC 101) requires that details of at least the last call received are stored in the "Received Calls" log (see chapter 1).

Channel 13

In U.S. coastal waters the following vessels must maintain a watch on VHF CH70 (if fitted with a DSC radio), CH13, and CH16 while the vessel is underway:

- power vessels of 65 feet, 6 inches (20 m) in length or over
- every commercial vessel over 100 U.S. tons (90.72 metric tons) and carrying one or more passengers for hire
- every commercial towing vessel 26 feet (7.9 m) in length or over
- every dredge and floating plant near a channel or fairway

Scanners alone cannot be used to meet this requirement. Two radios, one with two receivers, are required. When operating one of these vessels in the lower Mississippi River, you must maintain a listening watch on CH67 in place of CH13. In Canadian coastal waters, any vessel *required* to carry a VHF radio must also maintain a CH13 watch as well as a watch on CH70 and CH16.

One aspect of good watchkeeping is the ability of the sailing skipper to monitor simultaneously both the radio and what is happening on deck. A waterproof extension speaker in the cockpit is helpful and is particularly useful in rescue situations where the skipper is required to be everywhere at once. With a speaker in the cockpit, a member of the crew can be sent below to the VHF radio to carry out instructions while the skipper keeps control on deck.

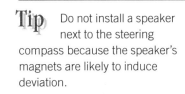 Do not install a speaker next to the steering compass because the speaker's magnets are likely to induce deviation.

Garbled Calls

Occasionally you'll receive a voice call but won't be able to determine who it's from or who it's for. Here is how to respond to these "garbled" calls:

1. **Unknown recipient.** When you receive a call but are unsure who it was addressed to, *do not reply*. Wait for the call to be repeated. Without this discipline, all the listening stations might reply, resulting in chaos. This highlights one problem with using the DSC "All Ships" call to contact an individual vessel whose MMSI number you don't know. A dozen vessels, all trying to determine whether the call is meant for them, could turn the

working channel into something as chaotic as the trading floor in the New York Stock Exchange.

2. **Unknown caller.** When your vessel receives a call that identifies your vessel by name, but you can't determine the identity of the calling station, make the following call (use your own vessel's name):

"Station calling *Papajon*—station calling *Papajon*—this is *Papajon* —say again—over."

Using a DSC-equipped radio to make the initial call removes this uncertainty—since the caller's MMSI number travels in the digital message—and is yet another reason to consider upgrading to DSC.

Unanswered Calls

Voice (Non-DSC) Calls

Continually repeating calls takes up valuable use of a channel and is an annoyance to everyone listening. For routine calls you can call up to a limit of 30 seconds and you may repeat the call at 2-minute intervals up to a maximum of three consecutive calls. After three call attempts you must wait at least 15 minutes before trying again. This does not apply to distress, urgency, or safety communications. Again, by upgrading to a DSC radio and using DSC to make the call, you will know that the call will be logged in the "Received Calls" log. So although you can't be totally sure that the call has been received until it has been acknowledged by voice, you can be sure that the DSC call covered a wider area than the equivalent voice call and therefore—provided the radio or radios called were monitoring CH70—the call has been received. This will be a blessing in busy areas where the constant prattle on calling channels is an annoyance to most boaters and an incentive to switch off the radio.

When a call goes unanswered, check that the controls on your unit are correctly adjusted as follows.

- the unit is powered up
- the volume is turned up—you won't hear a reply with the volume turned down
- the squelch control is adjusted only to reduce the background hiss and not mask the incoming signal
- the correct channel is selected
- the radio is *not* in "Dual Watch" mode
- high power is selected if low power has been unsuccessful

DSC Calls

Details of the DSC calls you receive are stored in the "Received Calls" log. The DSC controller can store details of at least the last call received (the minimum standard), but most radios have greater storage capacity. To check your logged calls, choose "Received Calls" and scroll through the list. If you wish to reply to the call, enter the MMSI number of the calling station (the other vessel or a land post) and make the DSC call in the normal way.

Call Planner

Before you press the transmit switch, assemble all the information you're likely to need, since most boaters don't use the radio often enough that all the procedures are second nature. To give yourself confidence, take a tip from telemarketers and use a call planner.

Tip Install the radio in a position where the controls are easy to use and read. Dim cabin lighting, salt-stained glasses, daylight glare, and postage-stamp-sized displays all conspire against easy use.

Tip Fill in your vessel's name, call sign (see glossary), MMSI number, phone company subscriber number, and phonetic spellings in permanent ink as shown in the example. Laminate the card so that it's reusable, then add the variable information using a nonpermanent pen.

➤ Call Planner

OWN VESSEL IDENTITY: G I Z Z Y   **MMSI:**   3 6 7 6 5 4 3 2 1

PHONETIC SPELLING: G O L F – I N D I A – Z U L U – Z U L U – Y A N K E E

CALL SIGN PHONETICS: W H I S K E Y   A L F A—O N E—T W O—F O E – W E R—T R E E

PHONE COMPANY SUBSCRIBER NO.: F L 3 2 1 4

CHANNEL FOR INITIAL CALL: CHANNEL FOR MESSAGE:

IDENTITY OF STATION YOU ARE CALLING: NAME:

MMSI: CALL SIGN:

MESSAGE

53

PART 3

USING YOUR VHF RADIO

CHAPTER 11

Distress Traffic

Channel	DSC	Voice	Single Frequency
70	✓		✓
16		✓	✓

In a book of this nature it would be impossible to describe the steps required to use each individual VHF-DSC radio available on the market. The manner in which information is displayed on the screens of various radio models may differ considerably. The following outlines the basic *principles* required to call for help and is no substitute for thorough study of the operator's manual that comes with an individual radio.

Distress is a situation in which, in the opinion of the master, a vessel, aircraft, vehicle, or person is in grave and imminent danger and requires immediate assistance. In other words, they need *help*. The key words are "grave and imminent danger," so running out of fuel or being lost does not normally qualify as a distress situation. However, running out of fuel and being swept rapidly onto rocks would constitute a distress situation as the vessel is in grave and imminent danger. A distress alert automatically gives immediate and absolute priority of communication to the vessel in distress and can only be sent with the authority of the master of the vessel. The voice signal "Mayday" is derived from the French *m'aider* and means "help me." Remember that a DSC alert call is just that—an electronic alert. It must be followed by voice communications.

Distress Alerting by DSC

A DSC distress alert is transmitted digitally on CH70 by lifting the spring-loaded cover and pressing the DISTRESS button at two different times. The digital alert is transmitted five times in succession to increase its chance of being received. The first one or two alerts may coincide with other CH70 traffic, but the speed of digital transmissions means that one of the remaining three alerts should be successful.

A DSC distress alert should include the vessel's MMSI number, its last known position, and the time (UTC) when that position was valid. If you interface the GPS or loran unit with your DSC controller, the current position and time will be included automatically. If this is not possible, the position and time will have to be programmed manually and updated at least every four hours but preferably hourly, when you update your position on the chart.

To update the position manually in your radio, follow the procedure in your operator's handbook (see page 27).

Distress Menu

The major problem in most distress situations is lack of time. Either the boat or crew is in a critical condition, or some part of the radio system is likely to fail imminently. This is why anything other than the most basic DSC radio comes with two distress alert options:

- an *undesignated* distress alert, where time is very limited. This is like the 911 call by phone, when the recipient has no idea of your problem until you begin to speak
- a *designated* distress alert, in which you can indicate the nature of the problem

Undesignated Distress Alert

All DSC radios will have the ability to send an undesignated distress alert (see the DSC menu options, pages 14–16). When there is no time to compose a comprehensive distress call:

1. Lift the cover, press the DISTRESS button once, and immediately release.
2. The screen (if available) will show DISTRESS: UNDESIGNATED.

```
37°11.3'N      76°10.2'W    13.20 UTC
DISTRESS: UNDESIGNATED   ⇕
PRESS DISTRESS TO TRANSMIT
REPLY   CH16
367987654                      25W
```

3. Now hold down the distress button for 5 seconds. The radio will count down from five. (Some SC 101 DSC radios require only a second push, not a hold-down, of the DISTRESS button. Other radios need a button push, plus activation of the transmit functions to send a distress alert—push the button, then key the microphone.)
4. You can cancel the alert during the countdown by pressing CANCEL.
5. After 5 seconds has elapsed, the alert is sent on CH70.

Designated Distress Alert

With a more sophisticated radio, and more time to compose the alert using the full distress menu, follow this general guide to the procedure:

1. Lift the cover and press the DISTRESS button only once. Do not hold down the button.
2. The screen will show DISTRESS: UNDESIGNATED.
3. SCROLL to access the "Designated Distress" list:

```
37°11.3'N        76°10.2'W    13.20 UTC

DISTRESS:  FIRE               ⇕
PRESS DISTRESS TO TRANSMIT

REPLY      CH16
367987654                     25W
```

   ◉ ABANDONING
   ◉ COLLISION
   ◉ CREW OVERBOARD
   ◉ DISABLED
   ◉ FIRE
   ◉ FLOODING
   ◉ GROUNDING
   ◉ LISTING
   ◉ PIRACY
   ◉ SINKING
   ◉ UNDESIGNATED

4. Once you have selected the appropriate distress category, simply push the DISTRESS button, key the mike, or press the DISTRESS button for 5 seconds, depending on the instructions in your manual. The alert will be transmitted at the end of the countdown.
5. You can cancel the alert at any point during the 5-second countdown by pressing the CANCEL button.

When the equipment at a coast station receives the DSC distress alert, you will get an immediate acknowledgment. If the distress alert goes unacknowledged, the DSC controller will automatically rebroadcast it at intervals of 3½ to 4½ minutes. This is another aspect of the GMDSS that could be better suited to small craft as in most cases a 20-foot (6.1 m) day cruiser will sink considerably faster than a supertanker.

You do not need to wait for the automatic repetitions as you can manually retransmit your distress alert *at any time* by pressing CANCEL, recomposing the distress alert and pressing the DISTRESS button again for 5 seconds. Doing this at 2-minute intervals is quite sufficient, otherwise the radio is unlikely to receive the DSC acknowledgment from the coast guard because the antenna will be busy transmitting the distress alert on CH70.

If another vessel provides you full assistance, cancel the DSC distress alert and tell the coast guard, otherwise they may assume the vessel has sunk and left you to become lunch for a passing shark.

Any distress alert must *be followed by voice communication on CH16. Allow 15 seconds for a DSC acknowledgment before transmitting your distress message on CH16.* This is because on most recreational craft radios with only one antenna, reception on CH70 is suspended while the distress message is transmitted on

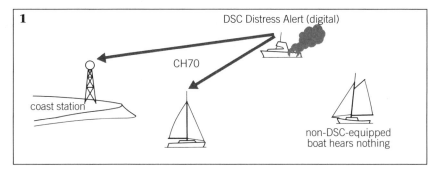

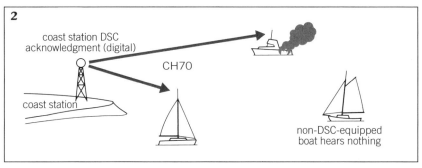

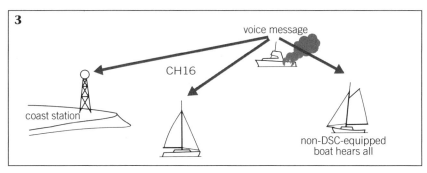

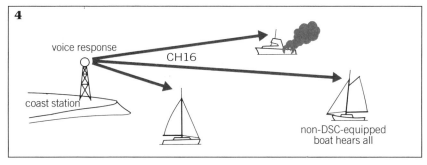

DSC Distress Alert. **1.** *Vessel on fire transmits DSC digital distress alert on CH70.* **2.** *Coast station transmits digital response on CH70.* **3.** *Distressed vessel transmits Mayday by voice on CH16.* **4.** *Coast station responds on CH16 by voice.*

CH16, and any DSC acknowledgement from the coast guard will not cancel the DSC distress alert. Fifteen seconds should give ample time for the distress alert to be acknowledged automatically.

The DSC acknowledgment of your distress alert will be displayed and prompt you to transmit your Mayday message on CH16.

The Distress Call and Message

Non-DSC Radios

If you don't have a DSC radio, follow the normal Mayday procedure set out below. An internationally recognized distress signal, the word *Mayday* is used to alert any vessel monitoring CH16. The distress call is a repetition of the word *Mayday* three times, followed by your identity (usually your boat's name) three times. As soon as you have transmitted the Mayday call, follow immediately with the message.

DSC Radios

After you have transmitted a distress alert on CH70, use the same voice procedure as distress alerts without DSC. Bear in mind that the DSC alert is simply a digital notification. You may question the need to repeat Mayday and your identity three times when you have already transmitted a distress alert on CH70, but for some time to come there will be many boaters who don't have DSC. Instead, they'll be listening on CH16 for three Maydays so, for the greatest chance of being rescued, it is still advisable to give the complete Mayday call and message after the DSC alert.

Once a DSC distress acknowledgment is received, the radio will automatically retune to CH16. When no acknowledgment is forthcoming within 15 seconds of the last repeated DSC alert, retune the radio manually, using the CH16 button.

Immediately transmit the distress message by saying the following slowly, clearly, and calmly:

┌─────────────┐
│ CALL   │   *Mayday, Mayday, Mayday*
└─────────────┘   *This is:*
                   Vessel name spoken three times; then your *MMSI number* (DSC only) or your *Call sign* or *Boat registration number*, spoken once.

┌─────────────┐
│ MESSAGE   │   *Mayday*—spoken once
└─────────────┘   *Vessel name* and *MMSI number* (DSC only), spoken once
                   The vessel's *Position* (see pages 38–39: by latitude and

longitude or distance and bearing from a well-known land-mark, or in any terms that will assist the rescue services. Include any information on vessel movement such as course, speed, and destination. Whether in a life raft.

The nature of *Distress* (sinking, fire, etc.)

Kind of *Assistance* desired

Number of *Persons* on board, including yourself

Any other *Information* that might help the rescue services, such as boat description, EPIRB activation, and so forth.

Vessel name and *MMSI number*, spoken once

Over

━━━━━

Adhering strictly to this order of information when transmitting ensures that the vessel can be located by rescue personnel, in case communication is lost. Unfortunately, in a distress situation, the first casualty is likely to be either the vessel's battery or antenna.

Tip To help get the message in the right order, use the mnemonic aid MIP-DAP-INO (see table). Each letter will help you to remember a key element of the message.

➤ The Distress Message

M	Mayday	Spoken once.
I	Identity	Vessel name and MMSI number, or call sign, or boat registration number
P	Position	Expressed as either latitude and longitude or a bearing and distance to a well-known landmark. Give the bearing first and distance second. It is difficult to determine distance accurately by eye so the rescue aircraft will fly to the charted object and fly along the bearing until you are sighted.
D	Distress	Sinking, on fire, man overboard, lee shore, etc. Whether in life raft.
A	Assistance required	Pumps, medical assistance, tow, and so forth.
P	Number on board	Total number of persons on board. Remember to include yourself.
I	Information	Information that will help the rescue, for example, the radio frequency of your activated EPIRB; a description of your vessel, etc.
N	Name	Vessel name and MMSI number, or call sign, or boat registration number.
O	Over	You want a reply.

Designated Distress Alert and Mayday Message

To do this, check with your owner's manual. Most radios will work something like this:

Your vessel, *Cinders*, is on fire.

Lift the cover and press the DISTRESS button once.

```
CH70
```

1. Scroll to access the "Designated Distress" list.
2. Scroll to "Fire."
3. Lift the cover again and press DISTRESS button for 5 seconds, or key the mike.
4. After 5 seconds the alert will begin transmitting.

```
37°11.3'N     76°10.2'W    13.20 UTC
DISTRESS: FIRE              ⇕
PRESS DISTRESS TO TRANSMIT

REPLY    CH16

367987654                        25W
```

Acknowledgment is received. Radio retunes to CH16 for the full Mayday voice call and message:

```
CH16
```

CALL: *Mayday, Mayday, Mayday*
           This is Cinders, Cinders, Cinders

MESSAGE:

M	(Mayday)	*Mayday*
I	(Identity)	*367987654*, Cinders
P	(Position)	*37°11.3′ N, 76°10.2′ W*
D	(Distress)	*On fire. Abandoning to life raft*
A	(Assistance)	*Require immediate assistance*
P	(People)	*Three persons on board*
I	(Information)	*EPIRB activated on 406 and 121.5 MHz*
N	(Name)	*This is Cinders*
O	(Over)	*Over*

Mayday Procedure Card

Commercial vessels are legally required to display a card close to the radio showing the distress procedure. This ensures that anyone on board is able transmit a coherent distress call. Recreational boaters will also find it useful, as radio procedure is the last thing likely to be remembered in an emergency. On the card include the vessel's name and call sign (if you have one; see glossary) spelled phonetically, the vessel's MMSI number, and the boat's registration number. The boat's registration details held by the authorities are particularly useful to the coast guard in an emergency. Laminate the card in plastic to make it waterproof. Below is an example that you can adapt with your own vessel details.

WARNING: If you get no response to your distress alert on CH70 or your Mayday call and message on CH16, rebroadcast your distress traffic (message) on any other channel you think will be monitored, such as CH09, CH13, or port operations.

▶ Mayday Procedure for DSC-Equipped Radios

1. Press DISTRESS button. Release, then press again for 5 SECONDS
2. After acknowledgment, the radio will retune to CH16. Press the button on the microphone. Remain calm. Say the following:

MAYDAY, MAYDAY, MAYDAY
This is *CINDERS, CINDERS, CINDERS*
MAYDAY 367987654, *CINDERS*

My position is ....(read position off the radio display or GPS)
Describe what's wrong........................(fire, sinking, crew overboard, etc.)
Immediate assistance required ....(or other if applicable)
Number of people ....(don't forget to include yourself)
Information to aid rescue: ....32-foot cabin cruiser, red hull, white deck
This is *CINDERS*
OVER

BOAT DETAILS
CINDERS: CHARLIE, INDIA, NOVEMBER, DELTA, ECHO, ROMEO, SIERRA
MMSI number: 367987654: THREE, SIX, SEVEN, NIGH-NER, EIGHT, SEVEN, SIX, FIFE, FOE-WER
REG. NO.: MA 12345: MIKE, ALFA, ONE, TWO, THREE, FOE-WER, FIFE
CALL SIGN: WA 4321: WHISKEY, ALFA, FOE-WER, THREE, TWO, ONE

Acknowledging Distress from a Ship Station

International rules state that *every station* is obligated to respond to a distress call made by another station. However, the introduction of GMDSS distinguished between digital distress alerts received on CH70 and Mayday calls received on CH16. Each is dealt with differently, and the procedure for dealing with each follows. These procedures apply to all vessels, large and small.

Acknowledging a CH70 DSC Distress Alert

SC 101 and class D DSC units do not allow you to respond to a CH70 DSC distress alert automatically using DSC, and while the following does not take away your obligation to answer a distress call, it does allow for the most practical assistance to be given.

When a distress alert is received, an audible alarm will sound. Silence the alarm, and while you are waiting for the DSC acknowledgment and voice message, do the following.

- *Make no transmission: all stations should cease transmitting and monitor VHF CH70 (DSC) and CH16 (voice).*
- From the DSC controller's screen, note and plot the casualty's position to determine your relative positions.
- Continue listening on CH16 until the distress alert has been acknowledged.
- Write down the message transmitted on CH16.

Depending on the location of the distressed vessel, monitor CH16 and take the following appropriate action.

Within Range of a Coast Station

If you receive an alert from a vessel and your vessel is within the radio range of a coast station, *do nothing initially, except monitor the situation closely for 5 minutes: only coast stations are permitted to acknowledge a DSC alert using DSC.* The coast guard system, when operational, is designed to be able to detect alerts at least 20 miles from shore. The DSC alert repeat time is between 3½ and 4½ minutes. If there is no response after 5 minutes or longer, contact the coast guard on CH16 and inform them of the distress situation. Once the alert has been acknowledged, write down the subsequent distress message and give your skipper its details.

Outside Range of a Coast Station

When you receive an alert and your vessel is outside the radio range of a coast station, *do nothing initially.* Wait 5 minutes for an acknowledgment, and once the alert has been acknowledged write down the subsequent distress message. If no acknowledgment is received, immediately inform your skipper and transmit a Mayday acknowledgment by voice on CH16:

1. *Mayday*
2. *Name* or *MMSI* of the vessel in distress, spoken three times
3. *"This is"*
4. *Name* of your vessel, spoken three times
5. *"Received Mayday."*
6. *State* the *Help* you can give and tell the vessel you will relay their distress call using the Mayday Relay procedure (see pages 67–68).

The cycle of five DSC distress alerts will take approximately 3 seconds and is repeated, randomly at intervals, for between 3½ and 4½ minutes. If your acknowledgment coincides with a repetition of the alert, wait until it is finished.

Alert the coast guard by any means possible.

If you can offer immediate assistance, for example, rescuing a person overboard, ask the distressed vessel to cancel the DSC distress alert and tell the coast guard by any means, so that they do not assume the person is still in the water. What you do after that depends entirely on the circumstances, but do try to maintain full contact with the coast guard.

Tip It's important always to keep a pencil and notepad close to the radio in case you need to write down the details of a distress alert and message. You may be the only one to receive it.

What to do if you receive a DSC distress alert

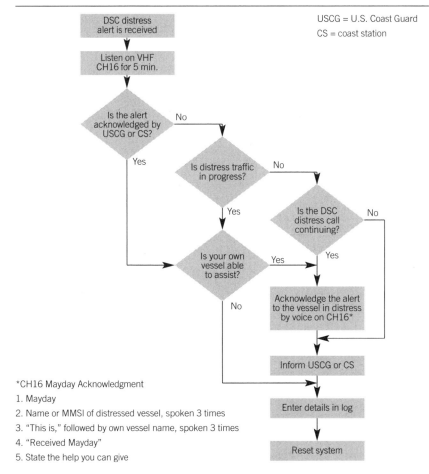

USCG = U.S. Coast Guard
CS = coast station

*CH16 Mayday Acknowledgment
1. Mayday
2. Name or MMSI of distressed vessel, spoken 3 times
3. "This is," followed by own vessel name, spoken 3 times
4. "Received Mayday"
5. State the help you can give

65

Acknowledging a Mayday Call on CH16

If you hear a Mayday call on CH16, prepare to take down the message that will follow, as you may be the only one to hear it. Quickly check the position of the casualty to see how close it is to you. You may not know whether the distressed vessel transmitted a DSC alert and so you must wait to see whether the coast guard is already aware of the situation or not. If it becomes apparent that you were the only vessel to hear the Mayday call, notify the coast guard and await further instructions.

Distress Relay

The digital distress relay option is only available to owners of DSC-equipped radios designed for commercial craft, because DSC radios designed for recreational craft use don't have this feature. On DSC, the only time a vessel can transmit a distress relay is if it sees a vessel in distress that cannot send its own distress call. This will be the case if you haven't heard radio distress traffic yet sight distress flares or see someone slowly raising and lowering their outstretched arms.

You must not relay any distress message that has already been acknowledged.

Distress Signals

Following is a list of the International Distress Signals you may see or hear while at sea.

- a distress alert sent on CH70 of a VHF DSC-equipped radio that remains unacknowledged
- the word *Mayday* by voice on the radio
- red flares, handheld or parachute
- orange smoke signal
- continuous sounding of a foghorn
- the signal transmitted by a Search-and-Rescue Radar Transponder (SART)
- flames on a vessel
- a person slowly and repeatedly raising and lowering arms outstretched to the side
- a ball over or under a square. The anchor ball raised above or below a flag is an example
- an orange flag with a black ball and square marked upon it
- SOS by sound or light. SOS in Morse is dot-dot-dot/dash-dash-dash/dot-dot-dot
- the signal code flags N and C
- flying the national ensign upside down

All but limited and specific types of vessels (those used on coastal waters, the Great Lakes, territorial seas, and those waters connected directly to them) must be equipped with distress signals approved by the coast guard. These include the following.

- ○ Red flares. Three that cover day and night use.
- ○ Orange distress flag. One, for day use only. It must be a minimum of 3 by 3 feet (0.9 by 0.9 m) with a black square and ball on an orange background. Tied across the cabin top, it is a particularly useful signal to a searching helicopter, as it identifies the distressed vessel in a crowd of other vessels.
- ○ Electric distress light that automatically flashes SOS. Night use only.

Under U.S. Inland Navigation Rules, a high-intensity white light flashing from 50 to 70 times per minute is considered a distress signal. These must not be used at sea; otherwise, a distressed vessel might be mistaken for a north cardinal mark.

Mayday Relay

A Mayday relay message makes it clear that the transmitting vessel is not in distress itself.

On DSC Radio

Neither an SC 101 radio nor a class D DSC controller should have the capability to send a DSC distress relay because one distressed vessel can generate hundreds of distress relay alerts. This is one lesson already learned from vessels equipped to GMDSS requirements whose DSC radios are capable of acknowledging a Mayday alert. With the exception of a small number of large vessels, all craft must make DSC acknowledgment calls direct to the coast guard.

To do this, check with your owner's manual. Most will work something like this:

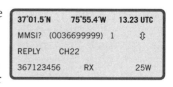

1. Select "Individual Call" from the DSC menu.
2. Use the coast guard's group MMSI number: 003669999 (U.S. only) either entered manually or selected from the "Directory."
3. Press ENTER or key the mike to confirm and again to send.
4. Once the coast guard has acknowledged the call and the radio has retuned to the working channel, transmit the Mayday relay call and message.

Once the coast guard has acknowledged your DSC alert, the radio will retune to a working channel selected by the coast guard. Transmit your call, prefixed "Mayday relay," spoken three times (see below). The word *re-lay* makes it clear that it is not your vessel in distress. Although few other vessels are likely to hear the Mayday relay message, once the coast guard has the information it will be retransmitted as a shore-to-ship distress alert relay to

- a specific ship
- a selected group of ships in a specific geographical area
- all ships

If you hear the coast guard distress relay and no other vessel responds, acknowledge receipt yourself.

On Non-DSC Radio

Apart from the DSC front end, the content of a Mayday relay call and message on a non-DSC radio is the same as the voice part of the DSC procedure:

Mayday Relay, Mayday Relay, Mayday Relay
This is: *Vessel Name*, **spoken three times**
Received **the following** *Mayday* **from:** *Name of vessel in distress* **and**
MMSI number (if known)
Details: **Give details of the Distress.**

CH16 Communications Control

During distress communications on CH16, silence is imposed on CH16 by a message issued by the coast guard, and no stations other than those directly concerned with the distress should use it. This is one of the reasons recreational craft are urged to use CH09 or an agreed working channel for inter-ship calling, rather than CH16. But there will always be someone who breaks the rules—that's why radio communications on CH16 are controlled. This control is achieved by using certain procedural words, as described below.

Silence Mayday

The coast guard station coordinating distress traffic and search-and-rescue operations keeps control of radio silence by use of the expression "Silence Mayday," pronounced *see-lonce may-day*. Stations that try to use CH16 and interfere with the distress or search-and-rescue traffic on CH16 will hear a Silence Mayday message similar to this:

Mayday
All Stations, All Stations, All Stations

Silence Mayday
This is Hampton Roads Coast Guard
Out

▬▬▬▬▬▬▬

Silence Distress

A station other than the station controlling distress communications can also impose silence on interfering stations by using the expression "Silence Distress," pronounced *see-lonce dis-tress*. For example, ship station *Gizzy* is aware of the Mayday situation hears another vessel, outside of the coastal radio range, break radio silence. *Gizzy* would transmit the following message to alert the other vessel to the Mayday situation.

▬▬▬▬▬▬▬

Mayday
All Stations, All Stations, All Stations
Silence distress
This is *Gizzy*
Out

▬▬▬▬▬▬▬

Prudence

Some distress situations can continue for a considerable time, which puts CH16 out of bounds for normal use. In some cases, limited communications may resume on CH16. This is announced by the word "Prudence" (French for "care" or "caution," and pronounced *pru-donce*). It means "restricted radio communications may commence" and the broadcast will follow on lines similar to that below. The name of the vessel to which the message applies is stated in order to identify a specific Mayday situation. At times, particularly in bad weather, simultaneous Maydays can occur, so naming each Mayday separately with the name of the vessel concerned is a means of differentiating one from another.

▬▬▬▬▬▬▬

Mayday
All Stations, All Stations, All Stations
This is Hampton Roads Coast Guard, Hampton Roads Coast Guard
271100 (date and time)
367987654, *Cinders*
Prudence
Out

▬▬▬▬▬▬▬

Silence Fini

Once the Mayday situation is over, the coast guard station controlling the search-and-rescue operations will broadcast a message containing the words

"Silence Fini," pronounced *see-lonce fee-nee* and meaning silence finished. This means that normal radio communications may resume. For example:

Mayday
All Stations, All Stations, All Stations
This is Hampton Roads Coast Guard, Hampton Roads Coast Guard
271130 (date and time)
367987654, *Cinders*
Silence fini
Out

Direction Finding

The coast guard shore stations, cutters, and search-and-rescue (SAR) aircraft have radio-direction-finding (RDF) equipment to locate distressed vessels. If the VHF radio continues to function, rescuers may request the distressed vessel to transmit a signal so that their RDF equipment can lock onto it. This is one of the major benefits of using a marine VHF radio rather than a cellular telephone in a distress situation because the SAR equipment cannot detect the frequencies used by cell phones.

When requesting a signal to be sent for detection purposes, the coast guard will ask you to say something. It may be similar to this:

Mayday
Cinders, Cinders
This is Hampton Roads Coast Guard, Hampton Roads Coast Guard
For direction-finding purposes on this frequency, key your transmit switch and hold it down for two periods of 10 seconds, then repeat your vessel name four times.
(A long count from 1 to 10 may be requested, as well.)
Over

The response from you should be

Mayday
Hampton Roads Coast Guard, Hampton Roads Coast Guard
This is *Cinders, Cinders, Cinders*
(10 sec PTT—10 sec PTT)
Cinders, Cinders, Cinders, Cinders
Over

Canceling a False Distress Alert

False distress alerts can overburden search-and-rescue services and may mask a genuine distress call. Any VHF station, whether DSC-equipped or not, can be subject to penalty if it does not immediately cancel an inadvertent or unnecessary distress alert.

DSC

DSC radio is a powerful tool, and because it's easy to use it's also easy to send a false distress alert, particularly when the operator is untrained. Inadequate training and the accidental misuse of poorly designed equipment has already seen a high number of false alerts by large ships, and this is likely to continue as more recreational vessels join the system. As a consequence, there is a real possibility that search-and-rescue services could be delayed in responding to a genuine distress.

If you inadvertently transmit a false DSC distress alert, do the following.

1. Switch off the radio transmitter immediately if you are still within the countdown period.
2. If the alert has been transmitted, address the following broadcast to all stations:

"All Stations, All Stations, All Stations"

"This is" (your vessel's name, call sign—if you have one—and MMSI number)

Position

"Cancel my distress alert of"—MMSI number, date, and time (UTC)

The coast guard can trace a vessel that transmits a false DSC distress alert. As long as the alert is reported and canceled immediately, the authorities will not normally take action against the mariner. However, in view of the serious consequences of false alerts and the strict ban on their transmission, prosecution may result from cases of repeated violations. To avoid making false alerts, do the following.

- Choose DSC equipment that is well designed, with a covered DISTRESS button and controls that suit your own needs, such as a clear display, large, illuminated buttons, (including numerical pad buttons), and an easy-to-use menu.
- Site the radio away from heavily used parts of the boat and the inquisitive fingers of children and crew.
- Ensure that only operators with appropriate training use the radio; otherwise, the skipper will be liable for the subsequent fine.
- Seek suitable training for yourself. See appendix 7, Contact Information.

Non-DSC

Although you cannot, as with a DSC unit, inadvertently hit the wrong button and transmit an automatic distress message, with voice VHF you might transmit a Mayday message but then realize that you can resolve the problem without further assistance. You have the same responsibility as a DSC owner to immediately cancel the alert.

If your Mayday has already been acknowledged by the coast guard, contact them directly on the appropriate channel (CH16 or CH22A) and explain the change in your circumstances. They will then broadcast a Mayday cancellation on your behalf.

If your Mayday has not yet been acknowledged, you must cancel the distress call and message yourself by using the format that follows.

"Mayday" (your vessel's name and call sign—if you have one)
"All Stations, All Stations, All Stations"
"This is" (your vessel's name and call sign—if you have one)
Position
"The time is" (state time using 24-hour clock)
"Silence fini"
Vessel name
"Out"

CHAPTER 12

Urgency Traffic

:··:
: VOICE CALL: PAN-PAN :
:··:

Channel	DSC	Voice	Single Frequency
70	✓		✓
16		✓	✓

The DSC urgency alert and voice call "Pan-Pan" (pronounced *pahn-pahn*) indicates that the station sending it has a very urgent message to transmit concerning the safety of a vessel or person. It is used where there is no *imminent* danger. The signal has priority over all other radio communications with the exception of distress, and can only be sent with the permission of the master of the vessel.

There is sometimes a fine line between a situation that is grave and imminent, and one that is urgent but not life-threatening. Only the skipper can make the distinction, and it must be remembered that an urgent situation may develop into a distress situation.

> **WARNING:** If you have a very basic DSC radio (e.g., SC 101), without the option of transmitting a preformatted urgency alert, *do not* opt for a distress alert. Transmitting false distress alerts incurs severe penalties. Instead, transmit an "all ships" call or call the coast guard direct using their group MMSI number: 003669999 (United States only).

Urgency Alerting by DSC

The major difference between a distress alert (Mayday) and an urgency (Pan-Pan) alert with a DSC radio is that position is omitted from the initial digital data sent in an urgency alert on CH70. It is displayed on the screen but isn't necessarily transmitted unless the unit has a menu option that allows position to be transmitted in all calls. Even then, existing DSC radios on commercial ships are unlikely to be able to decode and display the position in anything other than a distress alert. This is one of the primary shortcomings of the DSC system. A very basic DSC radio may not offer the "Urgency" option, so if you have one of these radios use the "All Ships" call instead.

Tip If you have a problem, the rescue services prefer to be advised about it promptly, preferably while you are still in open waters and while there is still daylight. Rescue services can accomplish in 1 hour of daylight what will take 8 hours in darkness.

To do this check with your owner's manual. Most will work something like this:

CH70

1. Select from the DSC menu "Urgency Alert" (if available) or "All Ships" or the MMSI number of the coast guard.
2. Press ENTER or key the mike to send. Do not push the DISTRESS button.
3. The radio will automatically retune to CH16.
4. The screen will prompt you to transmit your Urgency voice message.

Pan-Pan Message for DSC and Non-DSC Radios

This voice call is addressed to "all stations" or an individual coast guard station. The content of an urgency message (Pan-Pan) need not be as rigid or comprehensive as a distress message (Mayday) because it's assumed you have time to discuss your situation with the coast guard. If you don't have time to do this, then reconsider your decision to transmit an urgency alert rather than a distress alert. A guide to the message follows.

CH16	**Pan-Pan, Pan-Pan, Pan-Pan**	

"All stations" or individual coast guard station—spoken three times

"This is" followed by—MMSI number and the name, or call sign of your vessel—spoken three times.

Position, either latitude and longitude coordinates, or range and bearing to a land mark.

Details of Urgency situation.

Over.

```
37°11.3'N      76°10.2'W    13.23 UTC
SEND PAN-PAN ON CH16          ⇕
REPLY    CH16
303123456                    25W
```

Sample Pan-Pan Call

Transmit a DSC urgency alert following the steps on page 73. When your DSC receives a digital acknowledgment of your *alert,* it will prompt you to transmit your urgency (Pan-Pan) voice *message.*

CH16	*Pan-Pan, Pan-Pan, Pan-Pan*

All stations, all stations, all stations
This is 303123456, *Papajon, Papajon, Papajon.*
My position is 37°11.3′ N, 76°10.2′ W.
Steering failure. Drifting at 2 knots toward the shore.
Require an urgent tow.
Over.

Urgent Medical Advice

If you have an urgent message about the health of a person and require medical advice, you can seek this from a medic ashore. Make the DSC or voice call in the same way you would an urgency alert (see above). If you have transmitted your DSC urgency *alert* on CH70, once the alert has been acknowledged by the coast guard the radio will automatically switch to CH16 for your urgency voice *message*. State that you need urgent medical advice.

The coast guard will coordinate the medical assistance and will determine the response required, based on the information provided and the desires of the person or persons involved. If the sick or injured person needs direct advice from a specific doctor or medical service practitioner, the U.S. Coast Guard can usually make that connection.

There are several things that a responsible skipper can do beforehand that will save valuable time in a medical emergency:

- Make a list of all the medication carried on board the vessel and keep it close to the radio.
- Ask all members of crew for details of any health problems of which you need to be aware.
- Tell the crew of any medical condition you have, in case they have to summon medical assistance for you.
- Ensure that any crewmembers requiring essential medication have ample supplies with them *before* setting off. You don't want to be caught 50 miles off the coast with a diabetic in a coma because the insulin was left behind.
- Keep a very comprehensive medical kit on board. Don't forget to include a variety of seasickness remedies, equipment to deal with hypothermia, sunblock, a variety of painkillers, antiseptics, bandages, sticking plasters, and so forth.
- Seek thorough first-aid training.
- Ensure that someone else on board knows how to use the radio to call for help.

If you do have a medical emergency on board, try to get as many details as possible together about the casualty and the symptoms before making the call.

It's sometimes difficult to know whether a medical condition warrants a distress call or an urgency call. A distress call is appropriate if the life of the person is in imminent danger, as in the case of a heart attack, for example. In the case of severe abdominal pain, however, you may be unsure whether it is serious or simply the effects of last night's throat-ripping Tex-Mex take-out, so the appropriate call is "Pan-Pan" on CH16.

Receiving an Urgency Message

A vessel receiving a CH70 DSC urgency alert or a CH16 voice urgency call addressed to "All Ships" must listen to the message on CH16 and determine whether it is able to offer assistance. If it can, then the radio operator should contact the coast guard.

CHAPTER 13

Safety Traffic

....
: VOICE CALL: SÉCURITÉ :
....

Channel	DSC	Voice	Single Frequency
70	✓		✓
16		✓	✓
06		✓	✓
22A		✓	✓

The DSC safety alert followed by the voice call "Sécurité" (pronounced *say-curi-tay*) indicates that the calling station has an important navigational or meteorological warning to transmit. Safety messages are usually transmitted by the coast guard, commercial ships, and commercial towing vessels, and sometimes by recreational mariners.

Sending Safety Alerts

Safety Alerts by Coast Stations

The announcement of an upcoming safety message by the coast guard is made on CH16 using voice, and CH70 (after the year 2006) using DSC. This initial call simply alerts you to the working channel on which the safety message will be passed, which is generally 22A in the United States. In Canadian waters, listen carefully for the working channel number as several are available to the coast guard.

　　If you receive a safety alert on your DSC unit, press ENTER and the radio will automatically change to the working channel selected for the voice message. If you hear the alert on CH16, you must manually retune the radio to the working channel.

....
: CH16 :　　━━━━━
....　　Sécurité, Sécurité, Sécurité

Hello all stations.

This is Hampton Roads Coast Guard, Hampton Roads Coast Guard, Hampton Roads Coast Guard.

Marine Information Broadcast

OR Hurricane Advisory/Storm Warning/Thunderstorm Warning.
Listen on **CH22A.**
Out.

▬▬▬

▬▬▬
Sécurité, Sécurité, Sécurité
Hello all stations.
This is Hampton Roads Coast Guard.
Text of message.
This is Hampton Roads Coast Guard.
Out.

▬▬▬

Safety Alerts by Ship Stations: Passing a Safety Message to the Coast Guard

Not all safety messages are issued by the coast guard; a ship can also issue one. For example, you sight a large piece of lumber adrift and you're within radio range of the coast. You call the nearest coast guard station to allow it to rebroadcast the safety message with its more powerful transmitter, using the following general procedure.

CH70

1. Select "Individual Call" from the DSC menu.
2. Either manually enter "MMSI number" or select "Directory."
3. Press ENTER or key the mike to send alert. Do not push the DISTRESS button.

The radio will automatically retune to the selected working channel for the safety message to be passed by voice. The CH16 procedure that follows is the same for DSC and non-DSC communications.

CH16

▬▬▬
Hampton Roads Coast Guard, Hampton Roads Coast Guard, Hampton Roads Coast Guard.
This is 367123456, *Gizzy, Gizzy, Gizzy.*
I have a safety message for you.
Over.   *Gizzy.*
                          This is Hampton Roads Coast Guard.
                          Go ahead please.
                          Over.

Hampton Roads Coast Guard.

This is *Gizzy.*

My position is 37°11.3′ N, 76°10.2′ W.

I have sighted several large pieces of lumber drifting south, approximately a quarter-mile due west of my position.

Over.

"All Ships" Safety Call from an Individual Vessel

You are adrift in a shipping lane because your engine's water intake is blocked, and it will take you half an hour to get underway again. Because you pose a safety risk to other vessels, you must warn them, using either DSC or voice.

```
: CH70 :
```

1. Select "All Ships" call from the menu.
2. Select "Safety" (if the option is available).
3. Press ENTER or key the mike to send. Do not push the DISTRESS button.
4. The radio will automatically retune to CH16.
5. The screen will prompt you to transmit your safety message as follows.

```
37°11.3'N     76°10.2'W     13.20 UTC
SEND SAFETY MESSAGE ON CH16
REPLY     CH16
367123456                        25W
```

Once tuned to CH16 transmit your safety message.

```
: CH16 :
```

Sécurité, Sécurité, Sécurité

All ships, All ships, All ships.

This is 367123456, *Cosmos.*

My engine water intake is blocked.

My position is: 37°11.3′ N, 76°10.2′ W.

I request you give me a wide berth for the next 30 minutes.

Out.

Receiving a Safety Message

Vessels receiving a DSC safety alert announcing a safety message addressed to "all ships" must press ENTER on the DSC unit to allow the radio to retune to the selected channel, then monitor it for the message. Vessels hearing a Sécurité call on CH16 should retune manually to the selected working channel.

CHAPTER 14

Calling Another Vessel

Intership Channels

> ### Channels on Which to Call Other Vessels

KEY:
  GL = Great Lakes.
  EC = East Coast, including Newfoundland, Labrador, Atlantic Coast, Great Lakes, and Eastern Arctic.
  WC = West Coast, including Pacific Coast, Western Arctic, and Athabasca-Mackenzie Watershed areas.
  PC = Pacific Coast.
  AC = Atlantic Coast, Gulf, and St. Lawrence River up to and including Montréal.

Channel No.	Single Frequency	U.S.A.	Canada
06	✓	✓	✓ all areas
09	✓	✓	✓ WC, EC
10	✓		✓ AC, GL
11	✓		✓ PC, AC, GL
12	✓		✓ WC, AC, GL
67	✓		✓ all areas except EC
68	✓	✓	
69	✓	✓	
71	✓	✓	
72	✓	✓	✓ EC, PC
73	✓		✓ all areas except EC
74	✓		✓ EC, PC
78	✓	✓	
79	✓		✓ GL
80	✓	✓ GL	

Intership channels exist for passing messages concerned with ship's business, not for general chitchat between vessels. But defining *ship's business* can lead to hours of lively discussion! An inquest on yesterday's ballgame definitely does not qualify, whereas a recommendation to use Stop-It-Up for your leaking plumbing probably would. While no one is going to object to a little small talk, don't forget that you are hogging the channel and everyone else tuned to that channel can listen in on your conversation.

The channels listed in the accompanying table are all single-frequency working channels for noncommercial boats. Unless you use DSC to make the initial contact, the called vessel chooses the working channel, but if you can suggest a free working channel it will save time. Finding a free channel may be easier said than done, particularly in busy areas, so try by starting with the highest-numbered channel first and working downward. If you don't suggest a working channel, the called station will have to switch around the working channels, which, in turn, could lead to your losing contact with each other if the calling channel is in demand. It's not essential to use, CH16, or CH09 (U.S. only) for the initial call, as you can arrange to call direct on an intership channel. (Voice communications on CH70 have been disabled on new DSC radios.)

Collision Avoidance

Boaters often assume that a VHF radio is a useful tool for collision avoidance. They believe that because it allows two vessels to speak to each other, it offers an easy solution to a collision situation. Following are four reasons to treat this tactic with caution.

Identity

Identification of each other's vessel can be impossible, particularly in busy waters. You may be able to identify the name of a ship, but is that ship able to identify you? From a ship's bridge, one sailboat or powerboat can look much like another. Can you be absolutely sure that the ship knows which vessel it's trying to avoid? What's your escape route if the ship has made a mistake?

Collision Regulations

Under the rules of the road, vessels less than 65 feet, 7 inches (20 m) long must not impede the safe passage of vessels that can navigate only in a deep-water channel. So don't bother with the radio—obey the rules. A vessel costrained by draft has the right of way over most other vessels.

Speed

High-speed commercial traffic, with its tight timetables and business pressures, relies on navigation aids and has less time to discuss arrangements for avoiding collisions. In poor visibility, you may get your first sighting of a fast ferry when it's only a mile away, which, with a closing speed of 45 knots, will give you a little over 1 minute to decide what to do. It's unwise to assume that in poor visibility every fast vessel will slow down, and with this in mind, you should seriously consider postponing getting underway until conditions improve.

MMSI Numbers

Without the MMSI number of the other vessel, you will have to call on either CH16 or CH13 if the vessel is a commercial ship, or CH16 or CH09 (U.S. only) if it's a recreational craft. By the time you have established communication and confirmed each other's identity—ouch! It is much safer to observe and apply the rule of the road in ample time to avoid any chance of a collision.

Communications on Board

On-board communications using handheld equipment should be conducted on CH15 and CH17, as these channels are automatically restricted to 1 W of power to prevent interference on adjacent CH16. The usual form of an on-board call is to refer to the fixed radio as "*Vessel name* control" and each transportable radio as "*Vessel name* Alfa, Bravo, Charlie, " and so forth. For example:

Papajon Alfa, this is *Papajon* control, over.

Intership Calls

Sending DSC Intership Calls

CH70

1. Select the MMSI number from "Directory" or program the DSC unit manually with the MMSI number of the station you are to call.

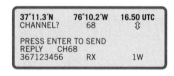

2. Select an appropriate working channel:

   - Recreational intership channels 06, 68, 69, 71, 78.
   - Recreational vessel to commercial ship: use CH67 or CH72.

3. Canadian vessels: check the bandplan for your area.
4. Set the radio to "Low Power."
5. Press ENTER or key the mike to transmit the call. Do not push the DISTRESS button.

Resist the temptation to use the "All Ships" call feature when the MMSI number of a vessel is unknown. The primary use of the "All Ships" call is to alert all vessels in the area to an urgency or safety situation. None of the stations that receive the call will know who the call was meant for, and unless it's designated as a safety call, will have to ignore it. In effect, it's the same set of circumstances as the "garbled" call, when the station is unsure of which vessel is being called. The rule is to not answer until it's clear exactly which station is being called.

Guide to Making a DSC Intership Call

	COSMOS CALLS GIZZY BY DSC	**GIZZY RECEIVES DSC CALL**
CH70	CHANNEL? 78 PRESS ACCEPT TO SEND ⇕ REPLY CH 78 367123456 RX 1W	CALL FROM [367123456] ON CH78 PRESS ACCEPT TO ANSWER ⇕ REPLY CH 78 367654321 RX 1W

Gizzy accepts the call.
Radio retunes to CH78.

CH78

Station calling *Gizzy*, Station calling *Gizzy*.
This is *Gizzy*.
Over.

Gizzy this is *Cosmos*.
We are 3 miles west of Gull Bay.
ETA 40 minutes.
What is your position and ETA?
Over.

Cosmos, *Gizzy*.
We are 2 miles southeast of Gull Bay, ETA 30 minutes.
We will see you there.
Over.

Gizzy, *Cosmos*.
Fine, have the beers ready.
Cosmos out.

Gizzy out.

Responding to a DSC Intership Call

When someone calls you, the radio will sound an alarm and display the call details on the screen. When you answer the call, your radio will automatically switch to the working channel suggested by the caller. If for some reason the suggested channel is inconvenient, you will have to make a fresh DSC call back to the calling station, inserting the working channel you wish to use. An alternative is to answer the call by voice and suggest the alternative channel.

The called vessel must start the conversation on the selected intership channel. If you know the name of the vessel from the MMSI number on the screen you should respond:

> *Cosmos*, this is *Gizzy*, over.

If you don't know the name of the calling vessel, respond like this:

> Station calling *Gizzy*, this is *Gizzy*, over.

Making a Non-DSC Intership Call

The FCC has designated CH09 as a supplementary calling channel for recreational craft in the United States. It is still permissible to use CH16, but if you do so you must be brief and no message may be passed, so it's wiser to leave CH16 to its other services and use CH09. You use CH09 to contact other vessels if you don't have a DSC radio or if you don't know the MMSI number of the vessel you wish to call. It's permissible to pass short messages on CH09, but don't take too long or you'll inconvenience other boaters. Remember, the U.S. Coast Guard does not monitor CH09.

"Compulsory" ships now monitor CH70 for DSC calls and CH16 and CH13 for voice calls. To call a ship, use CH16 then pass the message on a working channel. If your radio has only one receiver you should monitor CH70 for calls if your radio has DSC capability, or CH16 if it doesn't have DSC. Canada will continue to use CH16 for intership calling.

Before diving for the microphone's PTT switch, plan your call. In this example, *Cosmos* is calling *Gizzy*.

1. Note down all the information required to make the call (see Call Planner, page 53).
2. Listen to the intership working channels to find one that is free for use, so that you can suggest it to the called vessel.
3. Select the appropriate calling channel on low power and speak:

Tip Try to arrange a call with another vessel at a predetermined time directly on an intership channel. This will eliminate the risk of losing the other station during channel switching and cut down on the use of radio channels.

> Yacht *Gizzy*, this is *Cosmos*, channel 78, over.

4. Remain on the calling channel for the reply. If you don't receive an answer, wait 2 minutes and try again. Radio rules state that you may only try three times, with a 2-minute interval between each call. After that, you must wait for 15 minutes.
5. If the called station replies and is happy with your suggested working channel, the reply will be

> *Cosmos*, this is *Gizzy*, reply channel 78, over.

6. You will then say,

> *Gizzy*, *Cosmos*, **78** *or simply* **Roger.**

7. Retune the radio and pass your message.
8. The called station picks up the conversation on the working channel:

> *Gizzy* , this is *Cosmos*. We are three miles west of Gull Bay . . .

9. When you have finished talking, each station signs "Out" to signal that there is nothing else to be said and that the channel is about to become free.

CHAPTER 15

Calling the Coast Guard

➤ Coast Guard Channels

Channel	DSC	Voice	Working CH	Single Frequency
70	✓			✓
16		✓		✓
22A			✓	✓

Coast Guard Services

The U.S. and Canadian Coast Guards have established Rescue Coordination Centers all along the coastline. These centers organize the helicopters and rescue vessels that are sent to aid any kind of vessel in trouble.

Operating a rescue service is expensive for the taxpayer and dangerous for the personnel involved, so it's the responsibility of every skipper to make sure that the boat and crew are able to undertake the intended voyage. Bear in mind, too, that rescue services aren't intended to provide "breakdown" services. Here are some suggestions to help you avoid becoming another statistic in the history of maritime rescue.

- Ensure that everything on board works properly.
- Take adequate supplies of food, water, and fuel.
- Take adequate spares for the parts that may fail, know how to fit them, and ensure you have the right tools on board.
- Know first-aid and emergency procedures.
- Listen to the latest weather forecast *before* setting out (see chapter 16, Weather Information).
- Know how to get the boat and crew safely to their destination.
- Don't cruise and booze.

Weather and Safety Information

The coast guard broadcasts coastal forecasts, storm warnings, and navigational warnings on U.S. and Canadian CH22A after an initial announcement on CH16. After 2006, these will be sent by DSC on CH70 as well. The working channel in Canadian waters will depend where you are, so listen carefully to the announcement on CH16. For times of these broadcasts, refer to an almanac. In general, these transmissions will include information vital to the maritime community operating or approaching the coastal waters of the United States, including Alaska, Hawaii, Guam, and the Caribbean. Weather warnings are transmitted as safety (Sécurité) broadcasts.

WARNING: If in doubt, don't go out.

Weather forecasts are produced by local National Weather Services forecast offices. In areas where the National Oceanic and Atmospheric Administration (NOAA) weather-radio broadcasts overlap with the U.S. Coast Guard's weather-broadcast schedules, the coast guard may elect to broadcast storm warnings only. See appendix 4 for the U.S. Coast Guard broadcast schedule. These broadcasts usually include navigational warnings.

If you use the sources listed in chapter 16, Weather Information, there's no excuse for going to sea without an up-to-date weather forecast. You should get a forecast at least 12 hours before your proposed departure, but a safety-conscious skipper will have also been monitoring the weather for the week beforehand. When it comes to boating, weather conditions are everything.

➤ Safety Message Broadcasts

Message Type	Broadcast Schedule
scheduled broadcasts	as scheduled
safety broadcasts	on receipt, repeated next scheduled broadcast unless canceled
urgent broadcasts	on receipt, every 15 minutes for 1 hour, repeated on scheduled broadcasts until canceled

Float Plans

Tell a reliable shore contact and an alternate your plans so that if you become overdue, he or she will raise the alarm. It is common sense to stay in touch with your shore-based contact or contacts and keep them informed of your movements. This will reduce panic if you don't turn up where and when expected. Good passage planning involves selecting a series of diversion ports in case something unexpected occurs, so ensure that your contact is given these as well. If you do become overdue, this information gives the coast guard a good basis for launching a search operation. The coast guard will require the following information:

The 2-Minute Tip

Fill in all the information that doesn't change for the season. Before each individual trip, take 2 minutes to add the missing details. If you become overdue, those 2 minutes may save your life.

o the geographical area you are traveling in
o the registration number and MMSI number (if applicable) of your vessel
o the name and description of your vessel
o the number of crew on board

This is best given in the form of a "float plan" that you leave with your shore contact. *Do not file the plan with the coast guard.* See the sample float plan.

Direction Finding

Each coast guard cutter is fitted with radio direction-finding (RDF) equipment, and coast guard land stations will have this service by 2006. The purpose of this equipment is to provide bearings of a vessel in distress by locking on to a vessel's maritime VHF signal. VHF radio signals travel out from their source in straight lines and by using the RDF equipment the coast guard can home in on an individual vessel. The rescue vessel will track

➤ SAMPLE FLOAT PLAN

Name of person reporting and telephone number:

Boat name:

Type:	Sail/Power	Length:	Color:
Make:		Registration no.:	MMSI no.:
Engine:	Yes	No	
No. of engines:		Fuel capacity:	

Survival Equipment:

PFDs	Flares	Mirror	Smoke signals
Food	Water	Paddles	Flashlight
Anchor	Raft/Dinghy	EPIRB	Handheld VHF radio

Radio: Yes No Type: Freq.:

Cellular phone number:

Automobile license:	Type:	Trailer license:
Color:	Make of auto:	Where parked:

Persons aboard: name, age, phone number:

Do you or any of the persons aboard have a medical problem? If so, what?

Trip expectations: Leave at: From: To:

Expected to return by:

Possible diversion ports:

Any other pertinent information:

If not returned by: (time) call the **COAST GUARD** or local authority.

Telephone numbers:

your signal on RDF as it approaches, and all you need do is follow their instructions. The system is unable to detect signals from a cellular phone, however, which is one of the reasons the coast guard advises having aboard and knowing how to use a marine VHF radio.

Routine Calls to the Coast Guard

If you're using a non-DSC VHF radio, calling the coast guard is simple. The coast guard maintains a continuous watch on CH16, so ensure the radio is tuned to CH16, and select high power.

 Tip For instant use, program the U.S. Coast Guard group MMSI number 003669999 into memory location 1 and and your local coast guard MMSI number into memory location 2. (The Canadian Coast Guard does not currently have a group MMSI number, so store your local Canadian Coast Guard MMSI number in location 1.) This will enable you to use them quickly in an emergency. Coast guards maintain a continuous watch on CH16 for distress (Mayday), urgency (Pan-Pan), and safety (Sécurité) traffic and will keep watch on CH70 after 2006. Some U.S. Coast Guard vessels already have VHF-DSC aboard.

1. Call the appropriate coast guard station three times.
2. Give your vessel's name three times.
3. Say "Over."

The coast guard will respond and indicate the working channel for your message.

By 2006, the U.S. Coast Guard should have completed its upgrade of the VHF National Distress System to GMDSS specifications. It will then be using DSC. Each coast guard station has been issued with an MMSI number, and these are listed in appendix 6.

Contact the coast guard by DSC as described on page 48. Once your DSC unit receives an acknowledgment, the radio will automatically retune to CH22A so you can transmit your voice message.

Making a Routine DSC Call to the Coast Guard after 2006

You notice that the light on Crumps Bank buoy isn't operating and you decide to report it to the coast guard, using a routine call.

DSC Unit

CH70

1. Select "Individual Call" from the DSC menu.
2. Select "Manual."
3. Enter the MMSI of the Hampton Roads Coast Guard.

MANUAL MMSI? [003669933]

REPLY CH22A

367246813   25W

4. Press ENTER or key the mike to send. Do not push the DISTRESS button.

The radio will automatically retune to CH22A, as required in the acknowledgment sent by the coast guard, so that the message can be passed by voice. Follow the instructions below at CH22A.

CH16 **Non-DSC (Voice) Radio**

Hampton Roads Coast Guard, Hampton Roads Coast Guard, Hampton Roads Coast Guard.
This is *Oliver's Joy, Oliver's Joy, Oliver's Joy*.
Over.

> *Oliver's Joy*.
> This is Hampton Roads Coast Guard.
> CH22A please.
> Over.

CH22A Once you're tuned to CH22A, the message is the same for both types of call:

Hampton Roads Coast Guard, Hampton Roads Coast Guard, Hampton Roads Coast Guard.
This is *Oliver's Joy, Oliver's Joy, Oliver's Joy*.
Over.

> *Oliver's Joy*.
> This is Hampton Roads Coast Guard.
> Go ahead, please.
> Over.

Hampton Roads Coast Guard, *Oliver's Joy*.
The light on Crumps Bank buoy is unlit.
Over.

> *Oliver's Joy*, Hampton Roads Coast
> Guard.
> Thank you for the report.
> Hampton Roads Coast Guard.
> Out.

CHAPTER 16

Weather Information

Nobody should ever set out to sea without an up-to-date weather forecast from one of the sources listed here. It is probably the single most important factor in ensuring boating safety.

Weather-Wise Boating

Before you undertake any passage, it is vital to study the current and future weather. You need to consider the following.

- *What is the strength of the wind and its likely direction?* A gale on the nose is not for the faint-hearted; neither is running before a strong wind where the risk of a dangerous broach is ever present.
- *Where will waters be sheltered or exposed?*
- *What will be the likely sea state, particularly in relation to any shallow areas you are likely to encounter?* If the shallow area is open to the weather, dangerous waves will form in high winds.
- *What will be the direction of tidal currents in relation to the wind?* Wind moving in the same direction as currents will give a far smoother ride than wind blowing against the tide. Wind moving in the opposite direction to the tide drags the surface of the water into waves as it passes over and is apt to make the going uncomfortable and possibly dangerous.
- *What is visibility like?* Fog, mist, heavy rain, and spray will reduce visibility.

Where to Find Weather Forecasts

VHF Radio Forecasts

U.S. Coast Guard

The U.S. Coast Guard broadcasts coastal forecasts and storm warnings on CH22A after an initial announcement by voice on CH16. After 2006, *urgent,* nonroutine warnings will be announced on CH70 in addition to CH16. Local forecast offices of the National Weather Service produce these forecasts. Typical coverage is 20 miles offshore but can be significantly greater.

In areas where NOAA Weather Radio broadcasts provide complete overlapping coverage of the U.S. Coast Guard broadcast schedules, the coast guard may elect to broadcast storm warnings only and not routinely broadcast the National Weather Service forecasts. See appendix 4 for the U.S. Coast Guard broadcast schedule.

NOAA Weather Radio Services

The NOAA Weather Radio network provides computer-generated voice broadcasts of local and coastal marine forecasts on a continuous cycle. Coastal stations also broadcast predicted tides and current observations from buoys and coastal meteorological sensors operated by NOAA. The channel numbers given to VHF weather-broadcast frequencies (for example, WX1, WX2, and WX3) have no special significance but are often designated this way on the radio you buy. There are also other channel-numbering schemes in use. These are receive-only channels; you cannot transmit on them.

The NOAA Weather Radio network provides almost continuous coverage of the coastal United States, the Great Lakes, Hawaii, and the populated portion of the Alaskan coastline. Typical coverage is 25 miles offshore but may extend much farther in certain areas. Canada also has a continuous marine-broadcast service on WX1, WX2, and WX3.

Most VHF marine radios can receive NOAA Weather Radio broadcasts, but it's a good idea to carry a separate NOAA Weather Radio receiver on board so you can maintain a simultaneous radio watch on NOAA Weather Radio and on the marine VHF channels. An automated tone is transmitted to turn on compatible VHF marine radios automatically, but you must select an active NOAA Weather Radio channel in advance. This feature, known as Weather Alert, doesn't require you to listen to the weather channel.

A tone system incorporating newer technology, known as "specific area message encoding" (SAME), allows a receiver to sound an alert for certain specified weather conditions, or an alert for broadcasts concerning a limited geographic area, such as a county. The FCC is in the process of approving special SAME codes to delineate marine areas. At present, consumer-radio equipment (the kind available to amateur boaters) incorporating SAME issues alerts by geographic area only, and not for specific weather conditions.

Incidentally, if you're in transit, it's recommended that the SAME feature is *not* used. Otherwise, you'll need to continually reprogram the NOAA Weather Radio receiver as you move along the coast in order not to miss important warnings.

➤ NOAA Weather Radio Frequencies

Station	Frequency, MHz	Station	Frequency, MHz
WX1	162.550	WX5	162.450
WX2	162.400	WX6	162.500
WX3	162.475	WX7	162.525
WX4	162.425		

In Canadian waters, weather forecasts may be obtained from various sources. These include

- channels 21B and 83B on the Atlantic Coast and Great Lakes
- channels 21B and 39 (WX1) on the Pacific Coast
- Weatheradio Canada (Environment Canada), including VHF broadcasts in Vancouver, Toronto, Montreal, and Halifax
- regular AM and FM radio weather forecasts

Television

Television forecasts are for the most part biased toward land information and so are more concerned with sunshine, temperature, and rain than with wind. However, local television in coastal regions may give a boaters' forecast, so check the listings.

Weatherfax

Although this is not a VHF service, it does deserve mention because it's one of the ways to get comprehensive weather information while at sea. A number of weather charts are transmitted by radio facsimile over single-sideband (SSB) radio specifically for use by ships at sea. You will need a SSB radio and either a dedicated weatherfax receiver or a personal computer with weatherfax decoding software. The facsimiles include present surface analysis; planning forecasts up to 5 days; swell forecasts; sea temperature charts, and so forth, but you have to know something about reading weather maps to get the best from the service.

Navtex

Navtex provides an automated means of receiving weather information aboard vessels that are within about 200 miles of the shore. U.S. Navtex stations are operated by the coast guard, and their weather-broadcast schedule is detailed in the accompanying table.

Canadian vessels should consult an almanac or the *Admiralty List of Radio Signals*, volume 3, for the Navtex broadcast schedule.

Navtex receivers must be programmed with the correct Navtex station and subject identifiers in order to receive weather broadcasts. (For instructions on setting up a Navtex receiver, see the Navtex Systems section in chapter 22, Other GMDSS Equipment.)

Outside the United States, Navtex weather is broadcast with subject indicator B for meteorological warnings (which cannot be rejected by the Navtex receiver) and E for routine forecasts. However, because the U.S. National Weather Service normally includes meteorological warnings in forecast messages, U.S. meteorological warnings are broadcast using the subject indicator character E (see pages 118–19 for details).

➤ Broadcast Schedule for U.S. Navtex Stations

Station	Identifier	WX Broadcast Schedule (UTC)
Kodiak, Alaska[1]	J	0300, 0700, 1100, 1500, 1900, 2300
	X	0340, 0740, 1140, 1540, 1940, 2340
Astoria, Oregon	W	0130, 0530, 0930, 1330, 1730, 2130
San Francisco, California	C	0000, 0400, 0800, 1200, 1600, 2000
Cambria, California	Q	0045, 0445, 0845, 1245, 1645, 2045
Mariana Islands (Pacific)	V	0100, 0500, 0900, 1300, 1700, 2100
Honolulu, Hawaii	O	0040, 0440, 0840, 1240, 1640, 2040
Boston, Massachusetts	F	0045, 0445, 0845, 1245, 1645, 2045
Portsmouth, Virginia	N	0130, 0530, 0930, 1330, 1730, 2130
Savannah, Georgia	E	0040, 0440, 0840, 1240, 1640, 2040
Miami, Florida	A	0000, 0400, 0800, 1200, 1600, 2000
San Juan, Puerto Rico	R	0200, 0600, 1000, 1400, 1800, 2200
New Orleans, Louisiana	G	0300, 0700, 1100, 1500, 1900, 2300

1. Kodiak transmits both J and X Weather Bulletins.

Internet

This new and fast-growing way to get weather information is already widely used on land and will be increasingly used at sea as the technology becomes available.

Newspapers

Newspaper forecasts are at least 12 hours old by the time you come to read them, so they have limited value except for using the daily synoptic chart to see the weather trend.

CHAPTER 17

Making Phone Calls

Coast Radio Stations

The function of a coast radio station (CRS) is to link your VHF DSC or non-DSC radio with the land-based telephone system. In radio jargon, telephone calling is known as "public correspondence." The coast radio station service, which has been unavailable for several years, is undergoing an upgrading program that will include a VHF-DSC CH70 watch. As stations come back into service they will monitor CH70 for distress alerts and relay them to the coast guard. Service is now available in the Gulf of Mexico, with the rest of the country scheduled to come online by 2006. If you get into trouble and transmit a DSC distress alert, the CRS will inform the coast guard. It works just as it does at home when you make a 911 emergency call and the dispatcher informs the appropriate service. Canada no longer has a coast radio station network.

The coast radio station system is being modernized to keep pace with the changes required by the GMDSS and will provide boaters with automatic, private connections to the worldwide telephone network and will use digital selective calling (DSC). Commercial ships currently have the technology to use this service where suitable shoreside facilities are provided, and it is hoped that the next generation of VHF-DSC radios for recreational craft will offer it, as well. It will mean that operators equipped with the appropriate VHF-DSC radios will be able to make voice and data calls without operator assistance. Operator-assisted voice-telephone connections for owners of current-generation marine non-DSC and DSC radios will continue in limited areas along the coast.

The system uses towers 330 feet (100 m) tall or higher, sited close to the coastline, that will allow transmissions up to 100 miles offshore. Radio range on the West Coast and New England will be 100 miles and the rest of the U.S. coast 50 miles. Calls will be routed from these receiving towers over a fiber-optic network to one of two national call centers that will be manned 24 hours a day.

If you own a new radio that can dial directly into the land phone system, simply follow the instructions in the operator's manual. For those without this feature, follow the instructions on pages 95–96. Details of the working channels can be found in yachting almanacs, volume 1 of the *Admiralty List of Radio Signals*, and the documentation supplied by your system provider. To keep your subscriber and other information private on the ship-to-shore part of the conversation, the tower broadcasts a busy signal, so you needn't worry about divulging where mermaids have been sighted!

Phone Calls Step-by-Step

Using the Call Planner (see page 53), note down the following information.

- the name and working channels of the nearest coast radio station (see appendix 5)
- your phone service subscriber or account number (if you have one) or credit card number for billing purposes
- the telephone number you wish to call
- information required for the telephone conversation (MMSI numbers are not relevant to the telephone process except with DSC radios that contain the software to make automatic ship-to-shore and shore-to-ship telephone calls)

To make the call, follow these steps:

1. Select an appropriate public corespondence channel (see appendix 5) and listen for silence to indicate it is free for use.
2. If you hear the busy signal, switch to another working channel and try again.
3. Switch to high power and press the transmit button for 6 seconds. This will engage the working channel of the coast radio station. Release the switch.
4. You should then hear a recording that requests a second 6-second hold-down of the transmit button.
5. Remain tuned to the channel, and the operator will answer as soon as he or she is free.
6. Give the operator the details of your call (see above).
7. The operator will try to connect you.
8. At the end of the call, the link is severed when the receiver ashore is replaced.

Tip A phone call from a half-duplex VHF radio can confuse a listener ashore, so try to warn the people you call from your boat that they will need to say "over" when they want you to speak.

Shore-to-Ship Calls

If people ashore wish to call you, they will need to have some information about your vessel and your planned voyage before you set out to sea. For automated DSC calls, the only thing required will be the MMSI number, but for operator-assisted calls you need to leave the following details:

Tip Leave your float plan
with a reliable person
ashore whenever you go to sea,
and let friends and family know
who has this information (see
Sample Float Plan, page 87).

- your vessel's name
- the maritime phone service subscriber number (if you have one) and their toll-free number
- the name of the person being called
- the geographical area and likely position of your vessel

CHAPTER 18

VHF Radio versus Cellular Phones

VHF marine radios were designed with safety in mind. When you're in distress, your calls can be received not only by the coast guard but also by ships that may be in position to give you immediate assistance. A VHF marine radio also brings you storm warnings and other urgent marine information. The coast guard announces these broadcasts on VHF CH16. After 2006, they will also be announced on DSC on CH70. Timely receipt of such information may save your life. Additionally, your VHF marine radio can be used elsewhere in the world.

Cellular phones do provide the convenience of a simple, easy-to-use, inexpensive, private, and generally reliable telephone service to home, office, automobile, or other locations provided you aren't more than 10 miles from the coast. Cell-phone receiving antennas are designed for maximum land coverage and thus are tuned toward land, not the sea. In some places there is no cell-phone coverage at all. Additionally, you may not be able to use your cell phone outside the country, such as in the Bahamas, or outside your carrier's local service area without a special agreement.

Cell Phones on Boats

The coast guard does not advocate cell phones as a *substitute* for the regular VHF marine radio or the distress-and-safety systems in place around the coast. Nevertheless, cell phones can have a place on board as an *added* measure of safety.

Their limitations in an emergency are important to bear in mind:

- Cell phones are not waterproof or designed for the rough and corrosive marine environment. Try using your cell phone in the shower and see what happens!
- Cell phones generally cannot provide ship-to-ship safety communications, neither can you talk directly to rescue craft trying to find you unless they also have cell phones. For this type of communication you need a marine VHF radio.
- If you make a distress call on a cell phone, only the person you call will be able to hear you.
- Your cell-phone call will not have the priority access given to a VHF distress call.
- Most cell phones are designed for use on land so their coverage offshore is limited, and may change without notice.
- Cell-phone antennas are rarely placed on the coast, so if you're beneath a steep cliff your signal is unlikely to be picked up.
- Locating a cell-phone caller who is in trouble but can't give a precise position fix is difficult because the coast guard direction-finding equipment cannot detect cell-phone frequencies.
- Calling your mom to raise the alarm is not a good idea, since messages are likely to become muddled. "Pooped and sinking" offers all manner of misinterpretation to a nonsailor.
- Cell phones depend on charged batteries. A cell call will terminate when the battery is drained below a certain level.

Should you rely exclusively on a cell phone? No! There's no comparison between a cell phone and a VHF marine radio, with each providing a different service. The cell phone is best used for what it is: a link with shore-based telephones. A VHF marine radio is intended for communication with other ships or marine installations and is a powerful ally in an emergency.

There are no objections to your taking a cell phone aboard your boat, but if you are heading offshore, a cell phone is no substitute for a VHF radio. If you are within cellular range, it may provide a means of communication in *addition* to your marine VHF radio, and if you need to use your cell phone to report an incident at sea, the following guidelines should be used.

Note In some areas of the United States and in most areas of Canada, cellular service providers have established a special code (*CG) that will connect you directly—if you are in range—to a coast guard operations center. This service may work only with the carrier to which you have subscribed.

1. Use an external antenna.
2. Provide the emergency services with

   o the name and registration number of your vessel
   o your cell-phone number
   o your position
   o the nature of the problem
   o the number of persons on board
   o a brief description of the vessel
   o any other relevant information

3. Once you have reported the emergency, keep the line free for contact by the search-and-rescue services.
4. Conserve battery power as much as possible.
5. Try to keep the unit dry.

Here are some things *not* to do:

o Don't use a cell phone instead of a proper marine VHF radio.
o Don't hang up after talking to search-and-rescue services.
o Don't make other phone calls until the emergency services have finished their job.

CHAPTER 19

Port Operations and Marinas

Most harbor authorities and marinas use VHF and are assigned one of several channels reserved for port operations (note, however, that marinas do not have DSC capability). These are channels used to direct the movement of ships in or near ports, locks, or waterways. Appropriate almanacs give details of the working channels for individual harbors.

Vessel Traffic Services (VTS)

An increasing number of ports have Vessel Traffic Services (VTS) schemes. These are used chiefly to monitor commercial traffic in order to improve efficiency, safety, and environmental protection. VTS procedures are aimed primarily at commercial vessels, but recreational craft operators must check sailing directions to see whether they need to comply with specific regulations in specific harbors. In busy ports, particularly in poor visibility when the danger of being run down is at its greatest, recreational craft can learn the whereabouts of large vessels by monitoring the port's working channel.

Marinas and Noncommercial Harbors

Marinas and noncommercial harbors are also allocated one or more of the designated port operations channels. They monitor only their working channel or channels, so it doesn't help to call them on CH16. Details of working channels can be found in an almanac or appropriate cruising guides or piloting books.

A common reason for calling a marina is to book a visitor's berth for the night. Calling in advance ensures a suitable berth and you find out on which side of your boat to tie the warps and fenders. With a vessel that is wide, long, or deep-drafted, it's particularly important to check any entry restrictions with the dockmaster. Once a berth is allocated, repeat all the information back to the dockmaster to confirm you have understood his message. It's embarrassing to mistake P22 for D22 and find yourself aground, up a blind alley, in a fin-keeler that draws 6 feet (1.8 m), and feeling you should bow to the gathering audience.

Hailing a Marina

To make contact with a marina (marinas are not on DSC), complete your call planner with the following information.

- the name of the marina
- the marina's working channel
- your vessel's name (have the phonetics at hand, as well)
- the reason for your call: for example, you require a berth for one or more nights or need to refuel
- details of your vessel: length overall, beam, draft, multihull, and so on

Select low power and make your call.

CHAPTER 20

Marine Radio Legal Requirements in the United States and Canada

United States

Who Regulates Whom?

The **Federal Communications Commission (FCC)** regulates all use of radio on any recreational, commercial, state- and local-government, or foreign vessel in U.S. ports and waters. These regulations are contained in Title 47, Code of Federal Regulations, Part 80. Contact information for the FCC is in appendix 7.

The **National Telecommunications and Information Administration (NTIA)** regulates all use of radio aboard any federal-government vessel, including military vessels, in U.S. ports and waters. NTIA rules do not apply to non-federal-government vessels.

The **U.S. Coast Guard** enforces the radio requirement rules on commercial fishing vessels, foreign vessels in U.S. waters, survival craft, and vessels subject to the Bridge-to-Bridge Act—generally all vessels over 65 feet, 6 inches (20 m) in length.

The **International Telecommunication Union (ITU)** regulates all *use* of radio by any person or vessel outside U.S. waters. ITU rules affecting radio, which have treaty status in the United States, are published in the *ITU Radio Regulations*.

The **International Maritime Organization (IMO)** regulates the operation of most vessels outside U.S. waters, except warships. Most IMO radio regulations affect passenger ships and other types of ships of 300 gross tons (272.16 metric tons) and over. The IMO regulates the number and types of radio that must be carried and these rules, which have treaty status in the United States, are included in the Safety of Life at Sea (SOLAS) Convention.

Rules That Affect You

On 26 October 1996, the FCC eliminated the individual licensing requirement for "voluntary" vessels operating domestically that are not required by law to carry a radio.

Under the new rules, you don't need a license to use marine VHF radios, any type of EPIRB, any type of radar, GPS, or loran receivers, depth finders, or Citizen Band radio. An amateur license is required to use ham radio. Ships that use medium- and high-frequency single-sideband radio, satellite communications, or telegraphy must still be licensed by the FCC.

The following sections describe how the new rules affect the boating public.

Who Needs a Ship Station License?

You do not need a license to operate a marine VHF radio, radar, or an EPIRB aboard voluntary vessels operating domestically. The terms *voluntary* and *domestic* are defined below. Although a license is no longer required for these vessels, you *may* still obtain a license (and call sign) by applying to the FCC (see appendix 7, Contact Information).

> ## Geek-Speak
>
> A *station license* is an FCC license to operate marine VHF radio equipment. A *ship station license* is granted to vessels; a *marine utility station license* is granted to operate a handheld marine VHF radio from land. This book does not address VHF licenses required by coast stations.

Defining Voluntary Vessels

The term *voluntary ships* refers to vessels that are not required by law to carry a radio. Generally, this term applies to recreational craft or pleasure craft. In any event, *voluntary ships* does *not* apply to the following:

- cargo ships over 300 gross tons (272.16 metric tons) navigating in the open sea
- ships certified by the U.S. Coast Guard to carry more than six passengers for hire in the open sea or tidewaters of the United States
- power-driven ships over 65 feet, 7 inches (20 m) in length on navigable waterways
- ships of more than 100 gross tons (90.72 metric tons) certified by the U.S. Coast Guard to carry at least one passenger on navigable waterways
- commercial tow boats of more than 25 feet, 7 inches (7.8 m) in length on navigable waterways
- uninspected commercial fishing industry vessels required to carry a VHF radio

> ## Geek-Speak
>
> Most recreational boaters fall under the IMO's category of "voluntary ships."

Domestic Operation

Ships are considered to be operating domestically when they don't travel to foreign ports or don't transmit radio communications to foreign stations. If you travel to a foreign port (including Mexico, the Bahamas, and the British Virgin Islands), a license and an operator permit are required.

Getting a Ship Station License

In order to get a ship station license, request FCC Forms 159 and 506 and file them with the FCC (see appendix 7). The license the FCC will mail to you is valid for 10 years. Don't forget to sign and date your application and include any applicable fees—otherwise, it may be returned.

Renewing a Ship Station License

If you operate a marine VHF radio, radar, or EPIRB aboard a voluntary ship operating domestically, you aren't required to apply for a new license or renew your current license. Although a license is no longer required for these vessels, you may still renew your license and retain your call sign by applying to the FCC.

The FCC will send you a renewal application, FCC Form 405B, approximately 120 days prior to the expiration date of your license. If you don't receive this form within 30 days of the license's expiration date, obtain FCC Form 506 and use it to renew your license.

If you are on a vessel that requires a license, you must stop transmitting as soon as your license expires, unless you sent your renewal application to the FCC before the license expired. You may then continue to operate until the FCC acts on your application. You don't need a temporary permit, but keep a copy of the renewal application you send the FCC.

Expired Licenses

If your ship station license has expired, you must complete FCC Forms 159 and 506 for a *new* station license. There is *no* grace period. You may use the temporary operating authority (FCC Form 506A) to operate your marine radio while your application is being processed.

Noting Changes

If you change your mailing address, legal name, boat's name, ship official number, or state registration number, you must notify the FCC in writing. No fee is charged. No action is required when you add or replace a transmitter that operates in the same frequency band.

Fleet Licenses

Under certain conditions, two or more vessels having a common owner or operator may be issued a fleet license for operation of all ship radio stations aboard the vessels in the fleet. This allows an applicant to file a single FCC Form 506 for multiple vessels. The total fee due for the fleet license, however, is the fee due for a single license multiplied by the total number of vessels in the fleet. You must retain a copy of the fleet license with the station records on each vessel.

Restricted Operator Permits

If you plan to dock in a foreign port, including the Bahamas, or if you communicate with foreign coastal or ship stations, you must have a *restricted radiotelephone operator permit* (sometimes referred to by boaters as an "individual license") in addition to your ship station license. However, you don't need an operator permit if both of the following conditions apply:

1. you plan to sail only in domestic or international waters without docking in any foreign ports and without communicating with foreign coast stations
2. your radio operates only on VHF frequencies

Note that a ship station license pertains to the *radio equipment* aboard a ship, while the restricted radiotelephone operator permit authorizes *a specific person* to communicate with foreign stations or use certain radio equipment.

To obtain a restricted operator permit, complete FCC Form 159 and file it with the FCC. You don't need to take a test in the United States to obtain this permit. The permit the FCC will mail to you is valid for your lifetime. Don't forget to sign and date your application, and include any applicable fees—otherwise, it may be returned.

DSC Radios

If you have a DSC radio, you must obtain a nine-digit maritime mobile service identity (MMSI) number and have it programmed into the unit before you transmit (see pages 17–18 and 28). Before you are assigned an MMSI, you'll be asked to provide certain information about your boat. It's important that you obtain an MMSI number, because the U.S. Coast Guard uses this information to help speed search-and-rescue operations.

In the United States, recreational boaters may obtain an MMSI number by contacting Sea Tow, Maritel, or BoatU.S. MMSI Program. In Canada all requests for MMSI numbers must be made through the Industry Canada Web site. (See contact information in appendix 7.)

Operating Procedures

Even if a station license is no longer required on the vessel you operate, you must continue to follow ITU operating procedures for calling other stations, maintaining a safety watch, and relaying distress messages as specified in the FCC rules and detailed in this book. You may identify your ship station over the air using your boat's name, MMSI number, FCC-issued call sign, the state registration number, or official number of your vessel.

Temporary Operation

You may operate your marine radio after you have mailed your application or applications to the FCC as long as you fill out, detach, and retain the temporary operating authority attached to the application form. Valid for 90 days after you mail your application to the FCC, the temporary operating authority should be kept with your station records until you receive your license or permit through the mail.

Lost Licenses

If you lose your license or permit, you must request a duplicate in writing from the FCC (see appendix 7). For a duplicate ship station license, you must include your name, your boat's name, your station call sign, and a completed Remittance Advice, FCC Form 159. There are no provisions for issuing duplicate restricted radiotelephone operator permits. If you need to replace a lost permit, you must apply for a new one, using FCC Forms 159 and 753. You will be charged a fee for a duplicate license or a new permit.

Selling Your Vessel

If you have no ship station license but do have an MMSI number, you will need to contact the authority that issued your MMSI number to update the registration details.

If you have a ship station license and sell your boat, you must send your license, marked "Cancel," to the FCC.

You cannot transfer your ship station license to another person or ship. The new owner cannot modify your license but must instead apply for a new license.

If you have a restricted radiotelephone operator permit, retain it for future use, since it's valid for your lifetime.

Portable Ship Station

If you are required to have a ship station license and can provide justification for the use of a single transmitter from two or more vessels, a portable ship station license may be issued, instead. This could authorize various types of marine radio equipment to be carried from vessel to vessel.

Handheld Marine VHF Radios on Land

You must have a special license, called a "marine utility station license," to operate a handheld marine VHF radio from land—a ship station license is *not* sufficient. You may apply for this license by filing FCC Form 503 with the FCC. To be eligible for a marine utility station license, you must generally provide some sort of service to ships, or have control of a bridge or waterway. Additionally, you must show a need to communicate, using handheld portable equipment, from both a ship and from coast locations. Each unit must be capable of operation while being hand-carried by an individual. The station operates under the rules applicable to ship stations when the unit is aboard a ship, and under the rules applicable to private coast stations when the unit is on land.

Your station and your station records (station license and operator license or permit, if required) must be shown when requested by an authorized FCC representative.

Rule Violations

If it appears to the FCC that you have violated the Communications Act or the radio rules, the FCC may send you a written notice of the apparent violation. If the violation notice covers a technical radio standard, you must discontinue use of your radio until you have had all the technical problems fixed. You may have to report the results of those tests to the FCC. Test results must be signed by the commercial operator who conducted the test. If the FCC finds that you have willfully or repeatedly violated the Communications Act or the rules, your authorization to use the radio may be revoked and you may be fined or sent to prison.

Canada

License Requirements

If you do not intend to operate your vessel in the waters of a country other than Canada and the United States, and the radio equipment on board is only capable of operating on frequencies that are allocated for maritime mobile communications, you won't need a ship station license. These criteria apply to all vessels including passenger ships, safety services, and vessels involved in government operations. If, however, you don't satisfy both of these criteria, you will need a license and will need to contact Industry Canada (see appendix 7, Contact Information).

No maritime radio equipment, licensed or unlicensed, can be used on land or in vehicles for personal use in Canada. The intent of the maritime mobile bands is to provide safety communications to vessels. In the case of marinas or yacht clubs, maritime radio equipment may be used on land for communicating with ships or vessels, but radios for this type of operation will need a radio license.

Even if you don't need a ship station license, your radio equipment still requires to be approved for use in Canada.

If you have a DSC-equipped radio, you will need to obtain an MMSI number. See pages 17–18 for an explanation of how to obtain an MMSI number in Canada.

Call Sign Regulations

Industry Canada is no longer issuing call signs to stations that don't require a radio license. Vessels that don't meet the license exemption criteria will be issued a license and a call sign after they make application to their local Industry Canada office.

If you were previously issued a call sign but no longer need a station license, the call sign is no longer valid and should not be used. Use the vessel's name for identification. Some vessels, such as kayaks, have no name so it is suggested that for identification you say "Kayak Surname" (your surname). This will provide the coast station with an easy method of retrieving the information you have filed with them.

Operator Certification

The radio operator certificate is still a requirement in Canada for anyone who may be operating maritime radio equipment, regardless of whether a radio license is required.

To get a certificate requires successfully completing an examination. The exam can be taken in any Industry Canada office or with an examiner accredited by Industry Canada. Your local boating association may be able to provide you with more information.

PART 4

THE GLOBAL MARITIME DISTRESS AND SAFETY SYSTEM (GMDSS)

CHAPTER 21

What Is the Global Maritime Distress and Safety System?

Marine radio has been the prime means of communication for shipping for almost a hundred years. Its use and evolution has increasingly reduced the number of ships lost, but it has been far from perfect and vessels still get into trouble. This is why the International Maritime Organization (IMO), the body that regulates shipping, developed and implemented the Global Maritime Distress and Safety System (GMDSS). The system was originally designed only for use by commercial vessels and was implemented worldwide early in 1999. It uses radios with digital selective calling (DSC) capabilities that can both call for help and contact other vessels automatically, using digital signals (see chapter 1). The GMDSS is now the only system in use for the world's commercial shipping.

The basic concept of the GMDSS is to provide vessels with at least two reliable and different means of calling for help. This enables search-and-rescue (SAR) organizations, and other vessels close to the vessel or person in distress, to respond rapidly to an accident. The system uses three principal elements, all of which are explained in greater detail elsewhere in this book. They are

- digital selective calling (DSC) features on VHF and SSB radios
- emergency position-indicating radio beacons (EPIRBs) using the Cospas-Sarsat satellite system
- satellite communications using the Inmarsat satellite system

GMDSS enables any vessel equipped with a suitable DSC radio to communicate directly with the shore and always be within radio range of assistance. The DSC unit's distress button can generate a distress alert that contains both the identity and position of the vessel—but the position must either be keyed into the radio manually or obtained automatically from a GPS or loran unit connected to the radio. In addition, DSC allows one vessel to contact another almost as if it were a normal telephone call, using its Maritime Mobile Service Identity (MMSI) number. These features reduce the load on the traditional calling channels and relieve the need for a continuous listening watch.

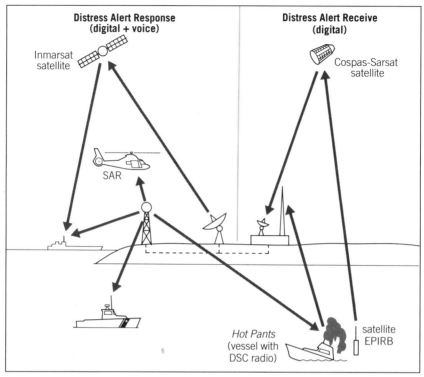

GMDSS Alerting System.

Hot Pants *hits the DISTRESS button on his DSC radio and also activates his satellite emergency position-indicating radio beacon (EPIRB). The DSC alert containing the boat's MMSI and position is relayed by the coast station antenna to search-and-rescue (SAR) organizations. The EPIRB signal is relayed by Cospas-Sarsat satellite to a shore-based satellite dish and decoded, and the information is relayed to SAR organizations. The receiving station transmits a digital response to the distressed vessel, and voice communications take over. Details of the Mayday are relayed by radio and Inmarsat satellite system to other vessels in the area.*

The choice of communications equipment for ships is laid down in the GMDSS regulations. All or part of the GMDSS regulations are a compulsory requirement for the list of U.S. vessels given on page 101.

The Canadian authorities have ruled that all commercial vessels over 26 feet (7.9 m) must carry a VHF-DSC radio.

The GMDSS recognizes that not all ships ply the seven seas, in fact some never leave coastal waters or the vast inland lakes. Therefore, the equipment that a vessel carries depends on the distance the vessel voyages from the coast rather than the tonnage of the vessel itself. The farther from the coast a vessel goes, the farther radio signals and other distress signals need to travel, and so a mixture of equipment is required.

Geek-Speak

Vessels compelled by regulations to carry certain radio equipment are known as "compulsory ships." Vessels not required to carry radio equipment are called "voluntary ships." Recreational craft fall into the latter category.

To put some order into the choice of suitable equipment the GMDSS splits the world's oceans into four separate areas:

- **Area A1.** Up to 50 miles offshore from a VHF coast station fitted with DSC—25 miles for voice—depending on the antenna height of the shore station. *This is where most recreational vessels operate.* VHF radio waves travel out from their source in straight lines and the antenna heights of the transmitting and receiving stations determine the distance at which a radio signal can be received.

- **Area A2.** From 50 to 300 miles distant of coast stations fitted with medium-frequency (MF-SSB) DSC features. These communicate with single-sideband (SSB) radios. Note that for most of the world, A2 will be approximately 100 miles during daylight, and more at night when radio propagation conditions are better. However, in some tropical areas such as the Caribbean Sea, A1 and A2 coverage may be nearly the same.

- **Area A3.** This lies within the coverage area of Inmarsat satellites—between 70°N and 70°S latitudes—and requires the use of satellite communications equipment or a high-frequency (HF-SSB) radio with DSC.

- **Area A4.** The remaining sea areas, using long-distance, high-frequency DSC radio signals. Again, an SSB radio is required.

The accompanying table lists the equipment included in the GMDSS, most of which will be carried only by commercial vessels, and for which strict regulations apply. However, because this book is for the recreational boater. I haven't, for example, explained the carriage requirements of a tanker. Therefore the accompanying table converts the IMO's recommendations into a realistic breakdown of the type of boating undertaken by recreational craft and makes equipment recommendations based on those criteria.

For recreational craft that venture only a few miles from the coast, there are only three pieces of equipment that you really need to consider:

- a DSC radio, which allows all radio watchkeeping to be automatic and digital calls to be transmitted. The radio itself maintains a constant watch on VHF CH70 and an alarm sounds when a call is received. The VHF-DSC radio is covered in detail in chapter 4. DSC applies equally to single-sideband (SSB) marine radios, but their use is beyond the scope of this book.

- an EPIRB that works on 406 MHz

- a NOAA weather radio

➤ Recommended Equipment

Area of Operation from Coast	Up to 5 miles	Up to 30 miles	Up to 60 miles	Up to 150 miles	Beyond 150 miles
handheld waterproof VHF radio; also for use in a life raft	✓	✓	✓	✓	✓
VHF-DSC fixed radio	0	✓	✓	✓	✓
406 MHz EPIRB with 121.5 MHz for homing and GPS for position	0	0	0	✓	✓
MF-DSC SSB radio			0	✓	✓
Inmarsat			0	0	✓
Navtex receiver		0	✓	✓	✓
search-and-rescue radar transponder (SART)		0	0	✓	✓
HF-DSC SSB radio					✓
VHF weather radio (not a GMDSS require-ment but very useful)	✓	✓	✓	✓	✓

   ✓   = *Recommended*
   0   = *Optional*
  (blank) = *Not required or recommended*

You might also consider the following additions.

- a Navtex receiver for navigational and meteorological warnings. (It helps stop you getting into trouble in the first place.) For recreational craft, this equipment is probably less important than a NOAA weather radio.
- a search-and-rescue transponder (SART). This transmits a signal that is received by another vessel's radar. It is used to locate a distressed vessel, lifeboat, or life raft.

How these technologies work is explained in the next chapter.

CHAPTER 22

Other GMDSS Equipment

EPIRBs

An emergency position-indicating radio beacon (EPIRB) is the closest thing boaters have to an instant prayer—the signal disappears heavenward and we wait to be saved. It's used as a second choice to a VHF radio for informing rescue services that a vessel or person is in distress. A radio is the first choice, because it allows you to explain your problem, but if you lose radio contact, or the vessel founders before a distress message can be sent, your EPIRB will send an alert via satellite to search-and-rescue (SAR) organizations. Satellites and EPIRBs form a vital part of the GMDSS.

Satellites and EPIRBs

Cospas-Sarsat is a dedicated, satellite-aided, search-and-rescue system designed to locate activated distress beacons transmitting on 406 and 121.5 MHz. Some older beacons also transmit on 243 MHz, but these no longer meet Cospas-Sarsat standards, and most companies have stopped making them. The 121.5 MHz frequency is also gradually being dropped by satellites. In fact, as of January 1, 2007, the 121.5/243 MHz EPIRB system will be scuttled in favor of the more modern 406 rescue alerting program. The first emergency position-indicating radio beacon (EPIRB) was developed to send emergency alerts to both orbiting Cospas-Sarsat satellites and aircraft flying international routes. Two frequencies were selected: 121.5 MHz for use with commercial aviation, and 234 MHz for use with military aircraft. When activated, such an EPIRB would broadcast a signal detected by the satellites, which in turn would eventually alert ground stations to the event. Though successful in saving lives, the program was plagued with troubles. These included frequency interference problems, inability to pinpoint the location of the event, and numerous "falsings."

To solve these problems, a new system was developed using more satellites, a higher 406 MHz frequency, and the ability to pinpoint location through the use of GPSs within the 406 EPIRBs themselves. The new 406s retained the older 121.5 MHz frequency, not for satellite alert but for homing by surface vessels. With 406 well established, the older satellites able to handle 121.5/243 MHz signals will go cold on January 1, 2009. In the meantime, though, 121.5 EPIRBs will no longer be manufactured or sold in this country after January 1, 2004. To allow for the internal battery life of those 121.5 EPIRBs sold before that time, use of such equipment will not be terminated until January 1, 2007.

On 406 EPIRBs, the 121.5 MHz homing signal will still be operational, but only as a surface rescue device, not as the satellite alert system. Here the 406 models will take over completely.

The satellites can detect and locate distress beacons worldwide. Once a distress signal has been received, the satellite relays it to a receiving station on earth, where the signal is processed to determine the location of the EPIRB. An alert is then relayed, along with location and other data, to a manned control center. In the case of a 406 MHz EPIRB, the identity of the vessel is determined from the registered identity code. The information is then passed to the appropriate rescue coordination center, which will initiate a search.

Selecting EPIRBs

121.5 MHz EPIRBs

These are the most commonly purchased and least expensive EPIRBs. The 121.5 MHz signals are best used for homing by search-and-rescue crews. (Actually, this class of EPRIB sends out two signals: 121.5 MHz, which is monitored by civilian aircraft, and 243 MHz, which is monitored by military aircraft.) Although they may be detected by satellite, there are limitations:

- A passing satellite cannot record and store 121.5 MHz alerts, so the satellite must be within sight of both the EPIRB and an earth-bound receiving dish simultaneously for detection to occur. This can be a big problem in large oceans.
- There is no vessel or personal identification encoded in the signals these EPIRBs send, which is a major disadvantage for you and the rescue services.
- Frequency congestion in the band used by these devices causes a false alarm rate of around 99.8 percent. Consequently, confirmation is required before a search-and-rescue operation can be mounted. That's not so good when you're being eyed up as lunch by Jaws Junior.
- EPIRBs manufactured before October 1989 may have design or construction problems that will prevent their working properly.
- Frequency instability, low power output (typically 75 mW), and poor alignment of the antenna by the user, all mean that the position of the EPIRB is ambiguous and at best is only accurate to within a 17-mile radius.

When the 121.5 MHz EPIRB works correctly, detection ranges from a beacon in the water will be as follows:

- to surface search-and-rescue craft, between 1 and 3 miles
- to helicopters at 2,000 feet (610 m), between 10 and 20 miles
- to high-altitude aircraft at a height of 30,000 feet (9,144 m), up to 200 miles. When an over-flying plane receives the signal, the pilot will radio its approximate position to the nearest control tower.

406 MHz EPIRBs

The 406 MHz EPIRBs operate exclusively with satellites, but they also include a 121.5 MHz homing signal that allows aircraft and rescue vessels to locate the distressed vessel quickly. The minimum response time is 30 minutes and the average is 1 hour, but it may take as long as 2 hours if the satellite has a lot of ocean to cross before it moves over a receiving dish on the ground. Position accuracy is to within 3 miles, but the next generation of 406 MHz EPIRBs will include distress information and GPS position fixing, as well. With GPS, accuracy can be within yards.

Tip If you need to replace a 121.5 MHz EPIRB, purchase a 406 MHz unit with 121.5 MHz for local homing only.

Other considerations when choosing a 406 MHz EPIRB include the following.

- If you select a float-free (category 1) device, you will need a mounting bracket with a hydrostatic release. Look for one that allows a simple quick change of the hydrostatic release mechanism, as it needs replacing more frequently than the battery inside the EPIRB.
- If the EPIRB is to be manually deployed (category 2), look for a release mechanism that cold, wet, panicky fingers can operate.
- Beacons should have a two-stage method of activation to avoid false alarms, but make sure they are easy to use with wet fingers.
- For nighttime use, a strobe light on the EPIRB is essential.

Care, Testing, and Use of Your EPIRB

The coast guard urges those owning EPIRBs to examine them regularly for watertightness, battery expiration date, and signal presence.

The batteries must be replaced by the date indicated on the label, and only a dealer appointed by the manufacturer should do this. EPIRBs use a type of lithium battery designed for long-term operation and low power consumption. If the replacement battery is not the approved type, the device won't operate for the required time—not something you want to discover after 24 hours in a damp, cold, lurching life raft.

Tip The coast guard recommends the 406 MHz EPIRB, preferably one with an integral GPS navigation receiver. A float-free EPIRB should be purchased if it can be installed properly.

For testing purposes, the FCC rules allow the following.

- A 121.5 MHz EPIRB may be turned on for 1 second during the first 5 minutes of each hour. By placing the EPIRB close to a normal radio tuned to 99.5 MHz FM, a signal should be detected.
- A 406 MHz EPIRB should be tested with the integral self-test function. It can also be tested inside a specially designed container. *Testing a 406 MHz EPIRB by allowing it to radiate outside of such a container is illegal and could result in a fine.*

When you're in distress, delay activating the EPIRB until you have alerted the coast guard by radio, if that's possible. If you can relay an accurate position, you may not need to activate the EPIRB.

WARNING: If for any reason an EPIRB is activated accidentally, the vessel should contact the nearest coast station or rescue control center and cancel the distress alert (see pages 71–72).

If you must abandon ship, take the EPIRB with you into the life raft, secure it, and then activate it. Remember, the satellite EPIRB is a one-way alert designed to be the system of last resort. The VHF radio is always preferred because its two-way communication allows you to speak directly with your rescuers.

Registering 406 MHz EPIRBs

One of the main advantages of buying a 406 MHz EPIRB is that each beacon has a unique code. When you purchase your beacon you will be given a registration card on which to supply details about yourself and your boat. If the EPIRB is properly registered, the coast guard will be able to take immediate action in an emergency, but if it is unregistered there is likely to be a 2-hour delay in getting a rescue mission underway.

The registration sheet you fill out and submit is entered into either the U.S. or Canadian 406 Beacon Registration Database. When your EPIRB is activated, your registration information will be sent to the

Tip When going boating, make sure you leave as much information about your intended voyage as possible with one or more of the contacts you list on your registration form (see the Float Plan section in chapter 15). Your life could depend on it.

appropriate coast guard center. One of the first steps they will take is to contact the owner or operator of the vessel at the phone number listed in the database, to determine if the vessel is really underway. This will uncover a false alarm due to accidental activation or EPIRB malfunction. If the vessel is underway, the coast guard may also be able to ascertain in this way the number of people on board and other vital information. If there is no answer at that number, or no information, the other numbers listed in the database will be called.

Other regulations on registration of your 406 MHz EPIRB are as follows.

- The FCC requires that you properly register your 406 MHz EPIRB. The coast guard enforces this rule.
- If you change your address, boat, or primary phone number, you must reregister your EPIRB.
- If you sell your U.S.-registered EPIRB, send written notification to Sarsat Beacon Registration (see appendix 7), or the coast guard may call you if it later becomes activated. Remind the purchaser to reregister the EPIRB.
- You no longer need a station license to purchase or carry an EPIRB.

If you need to register your EPIRB for a U.S. vessel and you don't have a form, call Sarsat Beacon Registration; mail or fax the completed forms back to them. If your vessel is of Canadian registry, mail your request to Canadian EPIRB Registry Director—you can also request the form by telephone—and the form will either be mailed or faxed to you. (See contact information in appendix 7.)

Search-and-Rescue Transponders (SARTs)

The purpose of a SART is to assist a search-and-rescue vessel or aircraft to locate survivors.

The SART is essentially a 9 GHz radar transponder that is mounted on an extendable pole and is activated by a vessel using 1.2-inch (3 cm) wavelength radar. Basically, the SART receives a radar signal and transmits another signal back to the sender. This signal is more powerful than the simple reflected signal provided by a radar reflector.

SARTs operate in the marine radar band. Most of the rescue aircraft worldwide have marine radar, but in the United States many coast guard and other search aircraft do not. All coast guard rescue aircraft are fitted with RDF units and are able to home in on 121.5 MHz signals from EPIRBs.

When the radar of a searching vessel activates a

Tip An alternative to a SART for pleasure craft is an emergency locating beacon that works on 121.5 MHz. Rescue services can home in on the 121.5 MHz signal. Hoisting a radar reflector also helps.

WARNING: Do not consider using a SART to replace a radar reflector or a radar target enhancer unless you are in distress. The signal from a SART is an internationally recognized distress signal, and any false alert could make you liable for a fine or prison sentence.

116

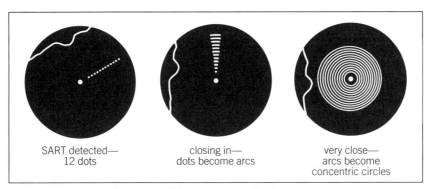

| SART detected—
12 dots | closing in—
dots become arcs | very close—
arcs become
concentric circles |

How a SART Appears on a Radar Screen

SART, 12 distinctive dots appear on the radar screen. As the searching vessel moves closer, the dots form arcs and finally, when the vessels are very close, the arcs become concentric circles.

Routinely check the SART for signs of damage and make sure the battery is replaced at the end of its life. In standby mode, a SART has a battery life of 96 hours and a life of 8 hours when it's transmitting, but it transmits only while it's under interrogation by a radar signal from another vessel. From a life raft to a searching aircraft

WARNING: Do not use a SART and a radar reflector together because the radar reflector may prevent a vessel's radar from detecting the SART.

the signal can be detected up to approximately 30 miles, but this range decreases to 5 miles for a searching ship. The signal range to a ship can be increased by extending the SART's pole to its maximum and by mounting the transponder as high up as possible so it can transmit farther over the horizon.

Navtex Systems

Navtex plays a vital part in the GMDSS by giving vital weather and navigation safety information that is designed to stop vessels getting into trouble in the first place. It is a low-cost, simple, automated system that provides a printout of essential navigation and weather information in English within approximately 200 miles of the shore. On U.S. recreational craft, it isn't as popular a choice of equipment as it is in other parts of the world, primarily because the NOAA weather radio is usually fitted instead.

Navtex information is transmitted on 518 kHz, which is not part of the VHF band of radio frequencies and therefore cannot be received on a VHF marine radio. The Navtex unit consists of a receiver permanently tuned to 518 kHz, and a screen or a continuous paper feed for printing the messages received. The receiver is designed to be left switched on continuously to automatically receive Maritime Safety Information such as navigation and gale warnings, weather forecasts, distress alerts, and so on. This can be a problem with the older paper-feed machines for obvious reasons. The unit can be programmed to receive only selected stations and categories of messages. In addition, a routine message already received won't be reprinted on subsequent transmissions, and messages won't be printed unless the received signal is strong enough to ensure good copy.

Interference between stations is avoided by allocating each Navtex shore station a different transmitting slot every four hours. Details can be found in *Boater's Almanacs*, NIMA Publication 117, and the *Admiralty List of Radio Signals*, volume 3.

The world is divided into NAVAREAS and the United States and Canada are in NAVAREAS IV (East Coast) and XII (West Coast). Each Navtex station has an identification letter that is programmed into the receiver (see the accompanying table). This ensures that you receive only the information relevant to your voyage.

Navtex stations in U.S. and Canadian waters use the characters found in the accompanying table.

➤ Navtex Station Identification Letters

Navtex Station	B1 Identity Letter(s)	Navtex Station	B1 Identity Letter(s)
Labrador, Newfoundland, Canada	X	San Juan, Puerto Rico	R
Sept-Îles, Québec, Canada	C, D	New Orleans, Louisiana	G
St. Johns, Newfoundland, Canada	O	Savannah, Georgia	E
Sydney, Nova Scotia, Canada	Q, S	Long Beach, California	Q
Yarmouth, Oregon	U, V	Point Reyes, California	C
Montreal, Québec, Canada	W, T	Cambria, California	Q
Thunder Bay, Ontario, Canada	P	Astoria, Washington	W
Wiarton, Ontario, Canada	H	Tofino, British Columbia, Canada	H
Boston, Massachusetts	F	Prince Rupert, British Columbia, Canada	D
Chesapeake, Virginia	N	Kodiak, Alaska	K
Bermuda	B	Honolulu, Hawaii	O
Miami, Florida	A	Guam	V

Navtex Subject Indicator Letters

The Navtex receiver uses a second set of the B2 subject indicator letters listed below to identify different classes of messages before deciding whether to accept or reject them. An asterisk follows messages that cannot be deselected.

A = navigational warnings*
B = meteorological warnings* (see note below)
C = ice reports
D = search-and-rescue information, and pirate warnings*
E = meteorological forecasts (see note below)
F = pilot service messages
G = DECCA messages
H = loran messages
I = OMEGA messages (note: OMEGA has been discontinued)
J = SATNAV messages (GPS, for example)
L = navigational warnings: additional to letter A (should not be rejected by the receiver)
V = Notices to Fishermen (U.S. only)
W = environmental (U.S. only)
X = special services: allocation by IMO Navtex Panel
Y = special services
Z = no message on hand

Note: The subject indicator letters B, F, and G are normally not used in the United States. Since the National Weather Service normally includes meteorological warnings in forecast messages, meteorological warnings are therefore broadcast using the subject indicator character E.

Setting Up Your Navtex:
10-Step Advice from the U.S. Coast Guard

1. If your Navtex is the older, paper-roll type, check that you have sufficient rolls on board.
2. Check that the paper is loaded into the receiver.
3. Switch the Navtex receiver on at least 4 hours before sailing. Better still, leave it turned on permanently, as this avoids the chance of losing vital information. This could, however, be a problem with paper-roll types.
4. Make sure that the operating manual is at hand.
5. Using your operator's manual and an index card, make yourself a handy guide for programming and auto-testing your vessel's equipment.
6. On the back of the guide, note the NAVAREAS in which you are likely to sail, their Navtex stations, coverage ranges, time schedules, and B1 characters. Place the card in a plastic cover and keep it with the equipment.
7. Program your receiver with the B1 character of the Navtex station in whose area you are sailing.
8. Program your receiver with the appropriate B2 characters to accept only those messages you want to receive. Characters A, B, and D are mandatory. It is recommended that you program all the rest,

except for navaid messages for equipment you don't have.

9. Take care not to confuse B1 and B2 characters. After programming always check the program status to ensure it's correct. Have another crew member double-check this.

10. If information is received incomplete or garbled, inform the relevant coast guard station, giving the time of reception (UTC) and your vessel's position. This will help to improve the system and anything that is safety-critical can be dealt with quickly.

CHAPTER 23

The Last Word: Training

Maritime communications have developed considerably since the *Titanic* disaster, and the VHF radio has saved countless lives across the world. But technology doesn't stand still, no matter how much we wish it would. Manufacturers will eventually cease the manufacture of non-DSC radios, and it will become increasingly difficult to find spare parts to keep the existing radios working. Once that time comes, as a safety-conscious skipper, you'll have to consider joining the digital age.

Unlike the majority of recreational boaters across the world, most U.S. boaters don't have to license their marine radios or undertake any mandatory training in their use. But this welcome freedom from bureaucracy also has a downside. GMDSS is still in its infancy and the current number of false alerts is high, due mainly to poorly designed commercial equipment and inadequate training of ship personnel who aren't career radio officers. Radio operation was once the province of the radio officer alone, but GMDSS, and its automatic watchkeeping, now allows for virtually any member of the ship's crew to use the radio. Once better-designed commercial equipment is installed in ships, and operator training is improved, the number of false alerts will drop. So, what will happen when untrained recreational boaters join the system in large numbers? I'll leave you to work that one out.

If you invest in a VHF-DSC radio, invest a little extra and seek some training—it might one day save your life and the lives of your crew. And, if it prevents your transmitting a false distress alert, it will also save your bank balance. For more information on training, see appendix 7, Contact Information.

Safe and happy boating!

APPENDICES

U.S. Maritime VHF Bandplan

➤ U.S. VHF Marine Radio Channels and Designated Uses

Channel	Frequency Operational Mode		Designated Use
	Single	Dual	
01A	✓		Port operations and commercial, VTS. New Orleans–Lower Mississippi
05A	✓		Port operations or VTS in the Houston, New Orleans, and Seattle areas
06	✓		Intership safety
07A	✓		Commercial
08	✓		Commercial (intership only)
09	✓		Boater calling. Commercial and noncommercial
10	✓		Commercial
11	✓		Commercial. VTS in selected areas
12	✓		Port operations. VTS in selected areas
13	✓		Intership navigation safety (bridge-to-bridge). Ships over 65 ft., 6 in. (20 m) in length
14	✓		Port operations. VTS in selected areas
15			Environmental (receive only). Used by class C EPIRBs
16	✓		International distress, safety, and calling. Ships required to carry radio
17	✓		State control
18A	✓		Commercial
19A	✓		Commercial
20		✓	Port operations
20A	✓		Port operations
21A	✓		U.S. Coast Guard only
22A	✓		Coast guard liaison and maritime safety information broadcasts
23A	✓		U.S. Coast Guard only

Channel	Frequency Operational Mode		Designated Use
	Single	**Dual**	
24		✓	Public correspondence
25		✓	Public correspondence
26		✓	Public correspondence
27		✓	Public correspondence
28		✓	Public correspondence
63A	✓		Port operations and commercial, VTS. New Orleans–Lower Mississippi
65A	✓		Port operations
66A	✓		Port operations
67	✓		Commercial. Bridge-to-bridge communications in lower Mississippi River
68	✓		Noncommercial
69	✓		Noncommercial
70	✓		Digital selective calling only. Voice transmission disabled on DSC radios
71	✓		Noncommercial
72	✓		Noncommercial (intership only)
73	✓		Port operations
74	✓		Port operations
77	✓		Port operations (intership only)
78A	✓		Noncommercial
79A	✓		Commercial. Noncommercial in Great Lakes only
80A	✓		Commercial. Noncommercial in Great Lakes only
81A	✓		U.S. Government only—environmental protection operations
82A	✓		U.S. Government only
83A	✓		U.S. Coast Guard only
84		✓	Public correspondence
85		✓	Public correspondence
86		✓	Public correspondence
87		✓	Public correspondence
88		✓	Public correspondence only near Canadian border
88A	✓		Commercial, intership only

"A" designates frequencies different from International Canadian Bandplan.

➤ U.S. Marine VHF Radio Channels and Allocation Rules

This table summarizes the portion of the FCC rules that applies to appropriate channel usage.

Message Type	Appropriate Channels
Distress, safety, and calling. Use this channel to get the attention of another station (calling) or in emergencies (distress and safety). This channel is also used as the distress-and-safety voice frequency when ships send a distress alert or make urgent or safety calls using DSC.	16
Intership safety. Use this channel for ship-to-ship safety messages, for search-and-rescue messages and ships and aircraft of the coast guard.	06
Coast guard liaison. Use this channel to talk to the coast guard after first making contact on channel 16. They will direct you to this or another working channel.	22A
Noncommercial. Working channels for *voluntary* boats. Messages must be about the needs of the ship. Typical uses include fishing reports, rendezvous, scheduling repairs, and berthing information. Use channels 67 and 72 only for ship-to-ship messages.	09,[1] 68, 69, 71, 72, 78, 79,[2] 80[2]
Commercial. Working channels for working ships only. Messages must be about business or needs of the ship. Use channels 08, 67, 72, and 88 only for ship-to-ship messages.	01,[3] 07, 08, 09, 10, 11, 18, 19, 63,[3] 67, 72,[4] 79, 80, 88[5]
Public correspondence (marine operator). Use these channels to call the marine operator at a public coast station. By contacting a public coast station, you can make and receive calls from telephones on shore. Except for distress calls, public coast stations usually charge for this service.	24, 25, 26, 27, 28, 84, 85, 86, 87, 88[6]
Port operations. These channels are used in directing the movement of ships in or near ports, locks, or waterways. Messages must be about the operational handling, movement, and safety of ships. In certain major ports, channels 11 and 12 are not available for general port operations messages. Use channel 20 only for ship-to-coast messages. Channel 77 is limited to intership communications to and from pilots.	01,[3] 05,[7] 12, 14, 20, 63,[3] 65, 66, 73, 74, 77
Navigational (bridge-to-bridge) channel. These channels are available to all ships. Messages must be about ship navigation, for example, passing or meeting other ships. You must keep your messages short. Your power output must not be more than 1 W. Most locks and drawbridges use these channels for their main working channels.	13, 67[8]
Maritime control. This channel may be used to talk to ships and coast stations operated by the state or local governments. Messages must pertain to regulation and control, boating activities, or assistance to ships.	17

Message Type	Appropriate Channels
Digital selective calling. Use this channel for distress-and-safety calling and for general-purpose calling using digital selective calling techniques. Voice disabled on DSC-equipped radios.	70
Weather. On these channels you may receive weather broadcasts of the National Oceanic and Atmospheric Administration. These channels are only for receiving. You cannot transmit on them.	WX1 162.55 MHz WX7 162.525 MHz WX6 162.500 MHz WX3 162.475 MHz WX5 162.450 MHz WX4 162.425 MHz WX2 162.4 MHz

1. Available for intership, ship, and coast general-purpose calling by noncommercial ships.
2. Available only in the Great Lakes.
3. Available only in the New Orleans area.
4. Available only in the Puget Sound and the Strait of Juan de Fuca.
5. Not available in the Great Lakes, St. Lawrence Seaway, or the Puget Sound and the Strait of Juan de Fuca and its approaches.
6. Only for use in the Great Lakes, St. Lawrence Seaway, and Puget Sound and the Strait of Juan de Fuca and its approaches. Channels 87B and 88B have been designated as the international AIS channels.
7. Available only in the Houston and New Orleans areas.
8. In the lower Mississippi River only.

Canadian Maritime VHF Bandplan

KEY	A: Frequencies different from those assigned to International Bandplan
	B: Receive only in Canadian Bandplan
	RX: Receive only; you cannot transmit on these channels
	PC: Pacific Coast
	EC: East Coast, including NL, AC, GL, and Eastern Arctic areas
	WC: West Coast, including the Pacific Coast, Western Arctic and Athabasca-Mackenzie Watershed areas
	AC: Atlantic Coast, including the Gulf of St. Lawrence and the St. Lawrence River up to and including Montréal
	GL: Great Lakes, including the St. Lawrence River above Montréal
	NL: Newfoundland and Labrador
All areas:	Includes East and West Coast areas

Channel	Frequency Operational Mode		Area	Designated Use
	Single	Dual		
01		✓	PC	Public correspondence
02		✓	PC	Public correspondence
03		✓	PC	Public correspondence
04A	✓		PC	Coast guard search-and-rescue
04A	✓		EC	Commercial fishing only
05A	✓		WC	Ship movement
06	✓		all areas	Intership. May be used for search-and-rescue communications
07A	✓		all areas	Intership. Commercial
08	✓		WC, EC	Intership. Commercial. Also operations in Lake Winnipeg area
09	✓		AC	Intership. Aircraft communications in maritime support operations
10	✓		AC, GL	Intership, safety, aircraft communications in SAR and antipollution
11	✓		PC, AC, GL	Intership, ship movement, and pilotage
12	✓		WC, AC, GL	Port operations and pilot information and messages

Channel	Frequency Operational Mode		Area	Designated Use
	Single	Dual		
13	✓		all areas	Exclusively for bridge-to-bridge navigational traffic
14	✓		AC, GL	Port operations and pilot information and messages
15	✓		all areas	Limited to 1 W power. On-board communications
16	✓		all areas	International distress, safety, and calling
17	✓		all areas	Limited to 1 W power. On-board communications
18A	✓		all areas	Intership. Towing on the Pacific coast
19A	✓		all areas except PC	Canadian Coast Guard only
19A	✓		PC	Various government departments
20		✓	all areas	Port operations 1 W maximum power
21A	✓		all areas	Canadian Coast Guard only
21B	✓ RX		all areas	Continuous marine broadcast service
22A	✓		all areas	Communications between coast guard and non–coast guard stations only
23		✓	PC	Public correspondence, also inland waters in British Columbia and Yukon
24		✓	all areas	Public correspondence
25		✓	PC	Public correspondence, operations in Lake Winnipeg area
25B	✓ RX		AC	Continuous marine broadcast service
26		✓	all areas	Public correspondence
27		✓	AC, GL, PC	Public correspondence
28		✓	PC	Public correspondence
28B	✓ RX		AC	Continuous marine broadcast service
60		✓	PC	Public correspondence
61A	✓		PC	Canadian Coast Guard only
61A	✓		EC	Commercial fishing only
62A	✓		PC	Canadian Coast Guard only
62A	✓		EC	Commercial fishing only
64		✓	PC	Public correspondence
64A	✓		EC	Commercial fishing only

(continued page 128)

Channel	Frequency Operational Mode		Area	Designated Use
	Single	Dual		
65A	✓			SAR and antipollution operations, GL. Towing, PC. Port operations, St. Lawrence River (1 W max.). Pleasure craft in the inland waters of Alberta, Saskatchewan, and Manitoba (excl. Lake Winnipeg and the Red River)
66A	✓			Port operations only in the St. Lawrence River–GL areas, max. 1 W power
67	✓		EC	Commercial fishing only
67	✓		all areas except EC	Communications with SAR and antipollution aircraft
68	✓		all areas	Marinas and yacht clubs
69	✓		all areas except EC	Intership
69	✓		EC	Commercial fishing only
70	✓		all areas	Digital Selective Calling for distress, safety, and calling
71	✓		PC	Intership
71	✓			Marinas and yacht clubs on EC and Lake Winnipeg
72	✓		EC, PC	Intership. Aircraft communications in maritime support operations
73	✓		EC	Commercial fishing only
73	✓		all areas except EC	Communications with SAR and antipollution aircraft
74	✓		EC, PC	Intership
75				Not available—guard band* for CH16
76				Not available—guard band* for CH16
77	✓		PC	Pilotage. Port operations, St. Lawrence River–GL areas, 1 W max.
78A	✓		EC, PC	Intership
79A	✓		EC, PC	Intership
80A	✓		EC, PC	Intership
81A	✓			Canadian Coast Guard use only in St. Lawrence River–GL areas
81A	✓		PC	Canadian Coast Guard antipollution
82A	✓		PC	Canadian Coast Guard use only
82A	✓			Canadian Coast Guard use only, in St. Lawrence River–GL areas

Channel	Frequency Operational Mode		Area	Designated Use
	Single	Dual		
83		✓	PC	Canadian Coast Guard use only
83A	✓		EC	Canadian Coast Guard and other government agencies
83B	✓ RX		AC, GL	Continuous marine broadcast service
84		✓	PC	Public correspondence
85		✓	AC, GL, NL	Public correspondence
86		✓	PC	Public correspondence
87		✓	AC, GL, NL	Public correspondence
88		✓	AC, GL, NL	Public correspondence
WX1	✓ RX		EC, PC	Continuous marine broadcast service
WX2	✓ RX		EC, PC	Continuous marine broadcast service
WX3	✓ RX		EC, PC	Continuous marine broadcast service

* guard band = an unused VHF channel that protects CH16 from spurious signals

International Maritime VHF Bandplan

Note that each country uses this International bandplan in slightly different ways.

➤ International Maritime VHF Bandplan

Channel	Frequency Operational Mode		USe
	Single	Dual	
01		✓	Port operations and ship movement. Public correspondence
02		✓	Port operations and ship movement. Public correspondence
03		✓	Port operations and ship movement. Public correspondence
04		✓	Port operations and ship movement. Public correspondence
05		✓	Port operations and ship movement. Public correspondence
06	✓		Intership
07		✓	Port operations and ship movement. Public correspondence
08	✓		Intership
09	✓		Port operations and ship movement
10	✓		Port operations and ship movement
11	✓		Port operations and ship movement
12	✓		Port operations and ship movement
13	✓		Port operations and ship movement
14	✓		Port operations and ship movement
15	✓		Port operations and ship movement
16	✓		Distress, safety, and calling
17	✓		Port operations and ship movement
18		✓	Port operations
19		✓	Port operations and ship movement
20		✓	Port operations and ship movement
21		✓	Port operations and ship movement
22		✓	Port operations and ship movement
23		✓	Public correspondence
24		✓	Public correspondence
25		✓	Public correspondence
26		✓	Public correspondence
27		✓	Public correspondence
28		✓	Public correspondence
60		✓	Port operations and ship movement. Public correspondence

Channel	Frequency Operational Mode	Use
	Single **Dual**	
61	✓	Port operations and ship movement. Public correspondence
62	✓	Port operations and ship movement. Public correspondence
63	✓	Port operations and ship movement. Public correspondence
64	✓	Port operations and ship movement. Public correspondence
65	✓	Port operations and ship movement. Public correspondence
66	✓	Port operations and ship movement. Public correspondence
67	✓	Intership
68	✓	Port operations and ship movement
69	✓	Port operations and ship movement
70	✓	Digital selective calling (DSC) only
71	✓	Port operations and ship movement
72	✓	Intership
73	✓	Port operations and ship movement
74	✓	Port operations and ship movement
75		CH16 guard band. May not be used
76		CH16 guard band. May not be used
77 ·	✓	Intership
78	✓	Port operations and ship movement. Public correspondence
79	✓	Port operations and ship movement
80	✓	Port operations and ship movement
81	✓	Port operations and ship movement
82	✓	Port operations and ship movement
83	✓	Public correspondence
84	✓	Port operations and ship movement
85	✓	Public correspondence
86	✓	Public correspondence
87	✓	Public correspondence
87B	✓	Automatic identification system (AIS)
88	✓	Public correspondence
88B	✓	Automatic identification system (AIS)

U.S. Coast Guard Weather Broadcast Schedule

Broadcasts are announced on CH70 and CH16. The broadcast itself follows on CH22A. The letter "Z" indicates time zone "Zulu," which is the same as Greenwich Mean Time (GMT) and Universal Coordinated Time (UTC). (See UTC in glossary for conversion formulas.)

First Coast Guard District	Broadcast Times
Group Southwest Harbor	1135Z, 2335Z
Group Portland	1105Z, 2305Z
Group Boston	1035Z, 2235Z
Group Woods Hole	1005Z, 2205Z
Group Moriches	0010Z, 1210Z
Group Long Island Sound	1120Z, 2320Z
Activities New York	1050Z, 2250Z

Fifth Coast Guard District	
Atlantic City	1103Z, 2303Z
Group Philadelphia	none
Baltimore	0130Z, 1205Z
Eastern Shore	0200Z, 1145Z
Hampton Roads	1230Z, 1120Z
Cape Hatteras	0100Z, 1055Z
Fort Macon	0103Z, 1233Z

Seventh Coast Guard District	
Group Charleston	1200Z, 2200Z
Group Mayport	1215Z, 2215Z
Group Miami Beach	1230Z, 2230Z
Group Key West	1200Z, 2200Z
Greater Antilles Section	1210Z, 2210Z
Group St. Petersburg	1300Z, 2300Z

Eighth Coast Guard District	Broadcast Times
Group Ohio Valley	none
Group Upper Mississippi Valley	none
Group Lower Mississippi Valley	none
Group Mobile	warnings only
Group New Orleans	1035Z, 1235Z, 1635Z, 2235Z
Group Galveston	1050Z, 1250Z, 1650Z, 2250Z
Group Corpus Christi	1040Z, 1240Z, 1640Z, 2240Z

Ninth Coast Guard District	
Group Buffalo	0255Z, 1455Z
Group Detroit	0135Z, 1335Z
Group Sault Ste. Marie	0005Z, 1205Z
Group Grand Haven	0235Z, 1435Z
Group Milwaukee	0255Z, 1455Z

Eleventh Coast Guard District	
Group Humboldt Bay	1615Z, 2315Z
Group San Francisco	1630Z, 1900Z, 2130Z (winter)
Group Los Angeles–Long Beach	0200Z, 1800Z
Activities San Diego	warnings only

Thirteenth Coast Guard District	
Group Seattle	0630Z, 1830Z
Group Port Angeles	0615Z, 1815Z
Group Astoria	0533Z, 1733Z
Group Portland	1745Z
Group North Bend	0603Z, 1803Z

Fourteenth Coast Guard District	
Group Honolulu	0500Z, 1700Z
Marianas Section	0900Z, 2100Z

Seventeenth Coast Guard District	
Communication Center Juneau[1]	0103Z, 0203Z, 0303Z, 0403Z, 1403Z, 1433Z, 1503Z
Air Station Kodiak	0133Z, 0233Z, 0533Z, 1433Z, 1603Z, 1803Z
Marine Safety Office Valdez	0115Z, 0133Z, 0715Z, 0733Z, 1315Z, 1333Z, 2115Z, 2133Z

1. Juneau controls 11 VHF stations remotely. To avoid interference, not all stations transmit during sched-uled time slots. All 11 stations broadcast as identical suite of National Weather Service products.

Maritel Coast Radio Station Channels

Note: At the time of writing, not all these channels are available in all areas. The system is planned to be completed by the end of 2002.

➤ Area	Channel	➤ Area	Channel
East Coast			
Maine		**Pennsylvania**	
Portland–Cape Elizabeth	24, 28, 87	Philadelphia	26
Massachusetts		**Delaware**	
Gloucester	25	Odessa	28
Hyannisport	28	Dover	84
Nantucket	85	Lewes	27
New Bedford	24, 26	Bethany Beach	86
Rhode Island		**Maryland**	
Providence	27	North Bay	24
Narragansett	84	Baltimore	25, 26
Connecticut		Cambridge	28
New London	26, 86	Point Lookout Ridge	26
Bridgeport	27	Ocean City	26
New York		**Virginia**	
Staten Island	28	Belle Haven	25
New Jersey		Virginia Beach	26, 27
Atlantic City	26	**North Carolina**	
Beach Haven	25	Morehead City	28
Cape May	24	Wilmington	26
Sandy Hook	24	**South Carolina**	
Ship Bottom	28	Georgetown	24
Toms River	27	Charleston	26

➤ Area	Channel	➤ Area	Channel

East Coast (cont.)

Georgia		**Florida (cont.)**	
Savannah	27	West Palm Beach	28
Florida		Ft. Lauderdale	8
Jacksonville	26	Miami	24, 25
Daytona Beach	28	Key Largo	27, 28
Cocoa Beach	26	Marathon	27
Vero Beach	27	Key West	26, 84
St Lucie	26		

Gulf Coast

Florida		**Louisiana**	
Naples	25	Hammond	85
Ft. Myers	26	Hopedale	85
Venice	27	Venice	27, 28, 86
Tampa Bay	24	Houma	86
Clearwater	26	Morgan City	24, 26
Port Richey	25	Erath	87
Crystal River	28	Lake Charles	28, 84
Apalachicola	28	**Texas**	
Panama City	26	Port Arthur	27
Ft. Walton Beach	28	High Island	85
Pensacola	26	Galveston	24
Mississippi		Arcadia	87
Pascagoula	27	Houston	26
Gulfport	28	Freeport	25, 27
		Matagorda	84
		Port O'Conner	24
		Corpus Christi	26, 28
		Port Mansfield	25

(continued page 136)

135

➤ Area	Channel	➤ Area	Channel

Mississippi River

Area	Channel	Area	Channel
Venice, Louisiana	27, 28, 86	Helena, Arkansas	27
New Orleans, Louisiana	24, 26, 87	Memphis, Tennessee	26
Hammond, Louisiana	85	Osceola, Arkansas	24
Convent, Louisiana	25	Caruthersville, Missouri	24
Baton Rouge, Louisiana	27, 87	Hickman, Kentucky	87
Melville, Louisiana	85	Cairo, Illinois	28
Natchez, Mississippi	84	Cape Girardeau, Missouri	24
Vicksburg, Mississippi	87	Dry Hill, Illinois	86
Lake Providence, Louisiana	25	St. Louis, Missouri	25
Greenville, Mississippi	85	Quincy, Illinois	26
Watson, Arkansas	25		

Arkansas, Illinois, Ohio, and Tennessee Rivers and Tenn-Tom Waterway

Arkansas River		**Ohio River**	
Little Rock, Arkansas	26	Paducah, Kentucky	26, 84
Watson, Arkansas	25	Evansville, Indiana	26
Illinois River		Tell City, Indiana	28
Chicago, Illinois	27	Gallipolis, Ohio	26
Joliet, Illinois	28	**Tennessee and Tenn-Tom**	
Ottawa, Illinois	26	Tennessee Ridge, Tennessee	85
Peoria, Illinois	28	Pickwick, Tennessee	86
Beardstown, Illinois	26	Muscle Shoals, Alabama	26
		Columbus, Mississippi	24

Great Lakes

Area	Channel	Area	Channel
Duluth, Minnesota	84	Rogers City, Michigan	28
Ontonagon, Michigan	86	Alpena, Michigan	84
Copper Harbor, Michigan	87	Tawas City, Michigan	87
Grand Marais, Michigan	86	Port Huron, Michigan	25
Sault Ste. Marie, Michigan	86	Detroit, Michigan	28
Port Washington, Wisconsin	85	Cleveland, Ohio	86
Charlevoix, Michigan	84	Buffalo, New York	28
Chicago, Illinois	27		

➤ Area	Channel	➤ Area	Channel
West Coast			
Washington		**Oregon (cont.)**	
Bellingham	28, 85	Newport	28
Port Angeles	25	Coos Bay	25
Camano Island	24	**California**	
Seattle	26	Santa Cruz	27
Tacoma	28	Santa Barbara	86
Tumwater	28	Redondo Beach	27, 85, 87
Oregon		**Hawaii**	
Astoria	24, 26	Haleakala, Maui	26
Rainier	28	Palehua, Oahu	27
Portland	26		

APPENDIX 6

U.S. and Canadian Coast Guard MMSI Numbers

➤ Group Location	MMSI	➤ Group Location	MMSI
United States			
Astoria, Oregon	003669935	Cape Hatteras, North Carolina	003669906
Boston, Massachusetts	003669927	Cape Hinchinbrook, Alaska	003669924
	003669991	Cape May, New Jersey	003669903
Brant Point, Massachusetts	003669902	Cape Yakataga, Alaska	003669924
Cape Arago, Oregon	003669911	*(continued page 138)*

137

➤ Group Location	MMSI	➤ Group Location	MMSI

United States (cont.)

Group Location	MMSI	Group Location	MMSI
Charleston, South Carolina	003669907	New Orleans, Louisiana	003669998
Chincoteague, Virginia	003669932		003669908
Chokoloskee, Florida	003669917	New York, New York	003669930
Corpus Christi, Texas	003669916	North Bend, Oregon	003669911
Fort Macon, North Carolina	003669920	Point Arena, California	003669909
Freeport, Texas	003669915	Point Conception, California	003669912
Ft. Pierce, Florida	003669919	Point Pinos, California	003669910
Ft. Stevens, Oregon	003669935	Port Angeles, Washington	003669904
Galveston, Texas	003669915	Port Isabel, Texas	003669916
Grand Isle, Louisiana	003669908	Portland, Oregon	003669934
Hampton Roads, Virginia	003669933	Portsmouth, Virginia	003669995
Honolulu, Hawaii	003669905	Point Higgins, Alaska	003669923
Humboldt Bay, California	003669909	Quillayute, Washington	003669904
Islamorada, Florida	003669919	St. Petersburg, Florida	003669917
Juneau, Alaska	003669922	San Clemente, California	003669913
Ketchikan, Alaska	003669923	San Diego, California	003669913
Key West, Florida	003669918	Sandy Hook, New Jersey	003669929
Kodiak, Alaska	003669899	San Francisco, California	003669926
Lena Point, Alaska	003669922		003669990
Long Beach, California	003669912	San Juan, Puerto Rico	003669992
Lualuaei, Hawaii	003669905	Santa Rosa, California	003669914
Marathon, Florida	003669918	Shinnecock, New York	003669936
Mayport, Florida	003669925	South Portland, Maine	003669928
Miami, Florida	003669997	Southwest Harbor, Maine	003669921
	003669919	Sullivan's Island, South Carolina	003669907
Mobile, Alabama	003669914	Valdez, Alaska	003669924
Monterey, California	003669910	Venice, Florida	003669917
Moriches, New York	003669936	Woods Hole, Massachusetts	003669902
Mullet Key, Florida	003669917	Yakutat, Alaska	003669922
New Haven, Connecticut	003669931		

➤ Group Location	MMSI	➤ Group Location	MMSI
Canada			
Comox, British Columbia	003160014	Québec, Québec	003160027
Halifax, Nova Scotia	003160016	Rivière-au-Renard, Québec	003160025
Inuvik, Northwest Territory	003160024	St. Anthony, Newfoundland	003160021
Iqaluit, Nunavut	003160023	Saint John, New Brunswick	003160015
Labrador, Labrador	003160022	St. John's, Newfoundland	003160020
Les Escoumins, Québec	003160026	Samia, Ontario	003160030
Montréal, Québec	003160028	Sydney, Nova Scotia	003160017
Placentia, Newfoundland	003160019	Thunder Bay, Ontario	003160031
Port aux Basques, Newfoundland	003160018	Tofino, British Columbia	003160012
Prescott, Ontario	003160029	Vancouver, British Columbia	003160010
Prince Rupert, British Columbia	003160013	Victoria, British Columbia	003160011

APPENDIX 7

Contact Information

United States

American Sail Training Association
(ASTA)
P.O. Box 1459
Newport RI 02840
401-846-1775
Fax 401-849-5400
tallships.sailtraining.org
asta@sailtraining.org
Training.

BoatU.S. Membership Services
880 S. Pickett St.
Alexandria VA 22304
800-395-2628; 703-461-4665
Fax 703-461-2845
www.boatus.com/

BoatU.S. MMSI Program
880 S. Pickett St.
Alexandria VA 22304
800-563-1536; 703-461-2840
www.boatus.com/mmsi
MMSI@BoatUS.com
Obtaining an MMSI identity number.

FCC Licensing
1270 Fairfield Rd.
Gettysburg PA 17325
888-CALL FCC (888-225-5322)
www.fcc.gov

GMDSS Task Force
GMDSS Implementation
7425 Elgar St.
Springfield VA 22151
703-941-1935
Fax 703-941-6154
www.gmdss.net
www.navcen.uscg.mil/marcomms/

Maritel
16 E. 41st St.
New York NY 10017
888-Maritel (888-627-4835)
Fax 888-MariFAX (627-4329)
Ship-to-shore phone communications.

Marlink (previously Comsat)
Telenor Satellite Services Inc.
6560 Rock Spring Dr.
Bethesda MD 20817
800-685-7898, 301-214-3100
Fax 301-214-7284
www.telenor-usa.com/
activations@telenor-usa.com
New global (including U.S.) provider
of mobile satellite communications, previously Comsat.

National Imagery and Mapping
Agency (NIMA)
4600 Sangmore Rd.
Bethesda MD 20816-5003
800-362-6289; 301-227-3149
Fax 301-227-3731
www.nima.mil/
navsafety@nima.mil
SafetyNET and Navtex.

National Safe Boating Council
P.O. Box 1058
Delaware OH 43015-1058
740-666-3009
Fax 740-666-3010
www.safeboatingcouncil.org/
nsbcdirect@safeboatingcouncil.org

National Weather Service
National Oceanic and Atmospheric
Administration (NOAA)
1325 East West Highway #14114
Silver Spring MD 20910
301-713-1677 ext. 128
Fax 301-713-1598
www.nws.noaa.gov/om/marine/
home.htm
marine.weather@noaa.gov
Marine weather, SafetyNET, and
Navtex.

NOAA-NWS Seas
4301 Rickenbacker Causeway
Miami FL 33149
305-361-4501
Fax 305-361-4366
seas.nos.noaa.gov
cook@aoml.noaa.gov
Weather observation system.

Public Safety and Wireless
    Telecommunications Bureau
Federal Communications
    Commission
445 12th St.
Washington DC 20554
888-CALL-FCC (888-225-5322);
    202-418-0680
www.fcc.gov/wtb/avmarsrv.html
mayday@fcc.gov

Sarsat Beacon Registration
E/SP3, Room 3320
FB-4 NOAA
5200 Auth Rd.
Suitland MD 20746-4304
888-212-7283
Fax 301-568-8649
EPIRB registration in the United
    States.

Sea Tow International
1560 Youngs Ave.
P.O. Box 1178
Southhold NY 11971
631-765-3660
www.seatow.com
MMSI registration in the United
    States.

U.S. Coast Guard
Navigation Center
7323 Telegraph Rd.
Alexandria VA 22310
703-313-5900
Fax 703-313-5805
www.navcen.uscg.mil/
nisws@smtp.navcen.uscg.mil
Loran and GPS.

U.S. Coast Guard HQ
USCGHQ (G-SCT)
2100 2nd St. S.W.
Washington DC 20593
800-842-8740 ext. 72860;
    202-267-2860
Fax 202-267-4106
www.navcen.uscg.mil/marcomms/
cgcomms@comdt.uscg.mil
Telecommunications.

U.S. Coast Guard HQ
USCGHQ (G-OPB)
2100 2nd St. S.W.
Washington DC 20593
800-368-5647; 202-267-1077
Fax 202-267-4285
www.uscgboating.org
uscgboating@comdt.uscg.mil
Boating safety.

USCG Amver (Vessel Reporting
    System)
USCG Battery Park Bldg.
New York NY 10004
212-668-7764
Fax 212-668-7684
www.uscg.mil/hq/osc/amver.htm
rkenney@batteryny.uscg.mil

U.S. Coast Guard Auxiliary
www.cgaux.org
Training.

U.S. Power Squadrons
P.O. Box 30423
Raleigh NC 27622
888-FOR-USPS (888-367-8777)
www.usps.org
Training.

International

Canadian Coast Guard
200 Kent St.
Ottawa ON
K1A 0E6, Canada
www.ccg-gcc.ca

Canadian EPIRB Registry Director
Search and Rescue
Canadian Coast Guard
Canada Building, 7th Floor
344 Slater St.
Ottawa ON
K1A 0N7 Canada
800-727-9414, 613-998-1559
Fax 613-998-9258
EPIRB registration in Canada.

Canadian Power and Sail Squadrons
26 Golden Gate Court
Scarborough ON
M1P 3A5, Canada
Toronto, 416-293-2438; all other
    areas, 888-CPS-BOAT
    (888-277-2628)
Fax 416-293-2445
www.cps-ecp.ca/html
hgg@cps-ecp.ca

Canadian Weather
321 St. Joseph's Blvd.
Hull PQ
K1A 0H3, Canada
800-668-6767; 819-997-2800
Fax 819-953-2225
www.ec.gc.ca/weather_e.html
enviroinfo@ec.gc.ca

Industry Canada
C. D. Home Building
235 Queen St.
Ottawa ON
K1A 0H5 Canada
613-954-2788
Fax 613-954-1894
info.ic.gc.ca
Licensing.

Industry Canada, Victoria District
    Office
318–816 Government St.
Victoria BC
V8W 1W9 Canada
Fax 250-363-0208
victoria.district@ic.gc.ca
http://strategis.ic.gc.ca/SSG/
    sf01032e.html
Obtaining and submitting MMSI
    number requests in Canada.

Sue Fletcher's Radio Web Site
www.learnradio.com
dsc@learnradio.com
+351-286-518022
Fax +351-286-518021
Online radio courses (beginning in
    2004).

Glossary

AIS. This Automatic Identification System is used by commercial shipping. It allows a vessel or coast station to interrogate another vessel's radio in order to learn the ship's position, course, speed, type of vessel, cargo, and so on. It may become available in the future to recreational vessels.

"All Ships" call. A DSC call automatically sent to and received by all DSC-equipped vessels that are monitoring CH70, or a voice call addressed to "All Ships."

bandplan. A plan showing the use of individual frequencies in a range of frequencies.

calling station. The station, either a vessel or a land post, that initiates a radio call.

call sign. Unique letter-and-number vessel identifier issued to vessels that are *required* to carry radio equipment and also to *voluntary* vessels calling at foreign ports. (See *voluntary fit*.)

coast radio station. CRS. A land-based service that provides ship-to-shore communications between marine VHF radios and shore telephones.

coast station. The radio station (literally, the equipment itself) at a land-based post, for example, a U.S. Coast Guard unit, a tug boat company or a fishing company. Compare *ship station*.

Cospas-Sarsat. A satellite-aided search-and-rescue system designed to locate EPIRBs transmitting on 121.5 MHz and 406 MHz.

DF. Direction-finding. The determination of a vessel's position by means of the reception of the radio signal transmitted by that vessel.

distress. A situation in which a vessel, vehicle, aircraft, or person is in grave and imminent danger. See *Mayday*.

DSC. Digital selective calling. Adjunct equipment that gives VHF (or SSB) radio the capability to transmit a digital signal to another radio station or stations.

DSC controller. The actual DSC unit that is either a separate unit or integrated into a VHF (or SSB) radio.

DTMF. Dual-tone multifrequency signaling. This is a direct-dialing feature on a radio that allows a direct connection to the telephone system ashore.

dual watch. A feature that allows a VHF radio to monitor CH16 and one other channel at the same time.

duplex. Radio communication that uses two antennas and a dual-frequency VHF channel. This allows two people to hold a normal two-way conversation like that used on a regular telephone.

EPIRB. Emergency position-indicating radio beacon. A beacon that indicates its position when activated; used in emergency situations.

FCC. Federal Communications Commission (U.S.). The federal government organization that manages the radio spectrum within the United States.

frequency. The number of vibrations or radio waves per unit of time. Frequency determines the pitch of a sound. It is reckoned in cycles per second with one up-and-down vibration or oscillation equaling one cycle. One cycle is called a "hertz."

GHz. One gigahertz is equal to 1,000,000,000 hertz. It is a measure of frequency and is the super-high-frequency radio wave used by equipment such as radar. From 3 to 30 GHz is described as "super-high" frequency, and 30 to 300 GHz is "extremely-high" frequency.

GMDSS. Global Maritime Distress and Safety System. A worldwide system for dealing with distress situations at sea.

GPS. Global positioning system. A satellite system enabling a GPS receiver to provide an accurate position for a vessel.

HF. High-frequency radio waves (3 to 30 MHz) used by radios that communicate over very long distances, hundreds even thousands of miles.

half-duplex. Radio communication that uses one antenna to switch between two frequencies on one channel. One frequency is used for transmitting and the other for receiving, which means that only one party can speak at a time. This system is used on some coast-station channels, notably those used for making phone calls.

Hz. Hertz. A unit of frequency. One hertz is one cycle or vibration in one second.

IMO. International Maritime Organization. The United Nations agency responsible for improving maritime safety and preventing pollution from ships.

Inmarsat. International Mobile Satellite Organization. A commercial organization that provides satellite communications to vessels between latitudes 70° North and 70° South.

ITU. International Telecommunication Union. The governing body for worldwide telecommunications.

kHz. Kilohertz. A measure of frequency. One kilohertz is 1,000 hertz per second.

marine utility station license. FCC license to operate a handheld marine VHF radio from land. Compare *ship station license.*

Maritel. Private marine telephone business that provided ship-to-shore telephone and data services.

Mayday. Distress signal. Origin French—*m'aider* (help me). Use in situation of grave and imminent danger. Commands highest level of attention. See also *Pan-Pan* (urgent signal) and *Sécurité* (safety signal).

MF. Medium-frequency radio waves (1,605 to 4,000 kHz) used by radios that communicate over medium distances, that is, up to 300 miles.

MHz. Megahertz. A measure of frequency. One megahertz is 1,000,000 hertz per second.

MID. Maritime Identification Digits. The GMDSS designation for the country-code portion of the MMSI number. For a shore station, the three digits of the MMSI after the two-digit shore station code comprise the MID; for a vessel, the first three digits of the MMSI comprise the MID.

MMSI number. Nine-digit Maritime Mobile Service Identity number that uniquely identifies an individual vessel, a group of vessels, or a coast station. A complete MMSI consists of an national code (see *MID*) and an individual station identity code; "00" always prefixes coast station MMSIs. The MMSI is broadcast digitally in an initial DSC contact and is used in the same way that a telephone number is used.

Navtex. Worldwide system of maritime safety information broadcasts in English, received as text on a dedicated receiver tuned to 518 kHz. Available up to 300 miles offshore.

NIMA. National Imagery and Mapping Agency (U.S.). A federal organization whose purpose is to "Provide timely, relevant and accurate Geospacial Intelligence in support of national security."

NMEA interface. The industry-standard method of connecting one piece of electronic equipment to another, for example, a GPS to an autopilot. NMEA stands for National Marine Electronics Association (U.S.).

NOAA. National Oceanographic and Atmospheric Administration (U.S.). A federal organization whose purpose is to "Describe and predict changes in the earth's environment and conserve and manage coastal and marine resources."

non-SOLAS. Vessels that need not comply with GMDSS regulations.

Pan-Pan. Spoken urgency signal concerning safety of vessel and/or people. Origin French—*en panne* (in difficulty). See *urgency traffic.*

PTT. Press-to-transmit switch. The switch on the microphone you press in order to transmit your voice communications.

portable ship station license. FCC license to operate a VHF marine radio from more than one vessel.

public correspondence. Ship-to-shore radiotelephone communications through a public coast radio station (marine operator).

radio check. Spoken test call that asks "What is the strength and clarity of my transmission?" Essentially, this request is asking for someone to respond to you, and in so doing indicates that your radio is working.

RDF. Radio direction-finding. See *DF* (direction-finding).

radio horizon. The maximum distance at which a particular radio signal can be usefully received.

Received Calls log. Notice of unacknowledged calls received by DSC radio.

restricted radiotelephone operator permit. FCC license that allows an operator to communicate via radiotelephone with foreign coastal or ship stations. Doesn't pertain to VHF communications. Also

145

called "individual license."

routine traffic. Routine radio communications. Compare *sécurité traffic* and *urgency traffic.*

RX. Radio shorthand for "receive." Used on the radio display to indicate that the radio is able to receive communications. Compare *TX.*

SAME. Specific area message encoding. Agencies that use this system, such as NOAA, can target vessels within one area, thus reducing unnecessary radio communications to vessels that cannot benefit from the information.

SAR. Search-and-rescue. The authorities that carry out search-and-rescue activities use this shortened version to describe what they do.

Sécurité. Safety signal. Origin French—*sécurité* (safety). Used to alert listeners to navigation hazards or ship movements. Compare *Mayday* and *Pan-Pan.*

sécurité traffic. Radio communication regarding safety issues. Voice communications begin with the prefix "Sécurité." Compare *routine traffic* and *urgency traffic.*

ship station. The radio station (literally, the equipment itself) on a vessel. Compare *coast station.*

ship station license. FCC license to operate marine VHF radio equipment aboard a vessel. Voluntary vessels operating within U.S. waters are no longer required to have ship station licenses for VHF operation. Compare *marine utility station license.*

simplex. Radio communication that uses the same frequency for transmitting and receiving. The limitation is that only one person can speak at a time but this mode of transmission allows both sides of a conversation to be monitored by a third party. For example, you can hear both conversations when the coast guard is speaking to a distressed vessel.

SOLAS. International Convention for the Safety of Life at Sea. This convention is the basis for many of the rules and regulations that govern the safety of vessels at sea.

squelch. A radio control that suppresses background interference. Without it, the signal you are listening for will be inaudible and lost in the background hiss.

station. See *coast station* and *ship station.*

traffic. Radio communications.

traffic routing. Details of a vessel's proposed passage, given to a coast radio station to ensure that radio traffic is broadcast by the most appropriate coast radio station.

TX. Radio shorthand for "transmit." Used on the radio display to indicate that the radio is transmitting communications. See also *RX.*

UHF. Ultra-high-frequency. Uses frequencies in the range of 300 to 3,000 MHz.

urgency. A situation that is serious but not yet grave and imminent.

urgency traffic. Radio communication of serious but not life-threatening issues. Voice communications begin with the prefix "Pan-Pan." Compare *routine traffic* and *sécurité traffic*.

USCG. United States Coast Guard.

UTC. Universal Coordinated Time. This was previously known as GMT (Greenwich Mean Time). UTC is the basis for all calculations of time, and it is the time displayed on a VHF-DSC radio.

The world is divided into zones that differ from the UTC time at the 000° meridian of longitude that passes through Greenwich, England. The 360° circumference of the earth is divided into 24 equal time zones of 15° longitude each that are measured either east or west from Greenwich. The United States and Canada are to the west of Greenwich, so when times there are compared to those at Greenwich they are earlier in the day. Eastern Canada is 4 hours earlier than Greenwich; U.S. Eastern Time Zone, 5 hours; Central Time Zone, 6 hours; Mountain Time Zone, 7 hours; Pacific Time Zone, 8 hours; Alaska Time Zone, 9 hours; and Hawaii, 10 hours.

To calculate UTC, take the local time and add the appropriate time difference to get UTC. For example, the local time in New York City is 0915 EST. Add 5 hours to get a UTC of 14.15. If the time addition is greater than 2400 hours, subtract 2400 to get the correct UTC.

To convert UTC to local time, take UTC and subtract the required hours of difference. For example, In Los Angeles, a UTC of 1300 minus 8.00 hours yields a local time of 0500 PST.

VHF. Very-high-frequency (30 to 300 MHz). The marine part of the VHF frequencies is from 156 MHz to 162 MHz.

voluntary fit. Vessels that need not comply with GMDSS requirements, for example, recreational vessels. No regulations exist that force leisure craft to carry any form of radio equipment.

VTS. Vessel traffic services. Maritime radio stations operated by large ports to deal with and control large vessels entering, leaving, and moving around inside the port.

watt. A unit of electrical power.

Making the Call: Quick Reference

Distress

DSC: Undesignated

With no time to compose the distress call, send an undesignated alert:

CH70

1. Lift the flap and press the DIS-TRESS button once and release.
2. The screen (if available) will show "Distress Undesignated."
3. Hold down the DISTRESS button for 5 seconds. The radio will count down from five. (On some radios, only a brief push of the button is required to send the alert.)
4. You can cancel the call at any time during the 5-second countdown.
5. After 5 seconds has elapsed the alert is sent on CH70.

DSC: Designated

With time to compose the distress alert, send a designated alert:

CH70

1. Lift the flap and press the DIS-TRESS button once and release.
2. The screen (if available) will show "Distress Undesignated."
3. Scroll to find the appropriate nature of distress.
4. Hold down the DISTRESS button for 5 seconds. The radio will count down from five.
5. The call can be canceled at any time during the 5-second countdown.
6. After 5 seconds has elapsed the alert is sent on CH70. (On some radios, only a brief push of the button is required to send the alert.)

Channel 16 Voice Call and Message

Once acknowledged, the radio will retune to CH16 where you will transmit the following:

⫶ CH16 ⫶   ▬▬▬▬

Mayday, Mayday, Mayday

This is . . .

Vessel name (spoken three times) and **MMSI** number (DSC only), or call sign, or boat registration number (spoken once).

▬▬▬▬

▬▬▬▬

Mayday (spoken once).

Vessel name and **MMSI** number (spoken once).

The vessel's *position*, by latitude and longitude or distance to a well-known landmark, or in any terms that will assist the rescue services. Include any information on vessel movement such as course, speed, destination, and whether you are in a life raft.

The nature of *distress* (sinking, fire, and so on).

Type of *assistance* desired.

Number of *persons* on board.

Any other *information* that might help the rescue services, such as hull color, **EPIRB**, and so on.

This is . . .

Vessel name.

Over.

▬▬▬▬

Mayday Relay

Using DSC

The class D DSC controller or SC 101 does not have the capability to send an automatic distress relay because one distressed vessel can generate hundreds of distress relay alerts. Recreational craft must make a DSC Urgency Alert to contact the coast guard, then transmit a Mayday relay message by voice on CH16.

⫶ CH70 ⫶

1. Select "Individual Call" from the DSC menu.
2. Use the coast guard's group MMSI number, 003669999, either entered manually or selected from "Directory."

37°11.3'N	76°10.2'W	13.23 UTC
MMSI? (003669999) 1		⇕
REPLY CH22		
367123456	RX	25W

3. Press ENTER to confirm and again to send. Do not press the DISTRESS button.
4. Once the radio has retuned to the working channel, transmit the Mayday relay call and message.

Voice

Apart from the DSC front end, a Mayday Relay on a non-DSC radio is the same as the CH16 part of the DSC procedure. Transmit the call, prefixed "Mayday Relay."

This is what to say:

CH16

Mayday Relay, Mayday Relay, Mayday Relay

This is . . . MMSI number (spoken once—DSC only) and name of your vessel (spoken three times).

Received the following Mayday from (Name of vessel in distress and MMSI number.)

Message begins: Transmit the message you wrote down, or details of the Distress.

Over.

Urgency

DSC

To make the DSC alert and call:

CH70

1. Select from the DSC menu "Urgency" (if available), "All Ships," or the coast guard group MMSI number.

2. Press ENTER to send. Do not press the DISTRESS button.
3. The radio will retune to CH16.
4. The screen will prompt you to transmit your Pan-Pan message.

Pan-Pan Call and Message for DSC and Non-DSC Radios

This call is addressed to "all stations" or an individual coast guard station. A guide to the format is as follows:

> **CH16**

Pan-Pan, Pan-Pan, Pan-Pan

All stations or individual coast guard station (spoken three times).

This is . . .

MMSI number and name, or call sign of own vessel (spoken three times).

Position, either latitude and longitude coordinates or range and bearing to a landmark.

Details of Urgent situation.

Over.

Safety

Calling the Coast Guard: DSC

> **CH70**

1. Select "Individual Call" from the DSC menu.
2. Either manually enter MMSI number or select it from "Directory."
3. Press ENTER to send alert. Do not press the DISTRESS button.

The radio will automatically retune to the selected working channel for the message to be passed by voice as follows:

> **CH22A**

Name of coast guard (three times).

This is (MMSI number and name) (three times).

Reason for call.

Over.

Calling the Coast Guard: Voice

> **CH16**

Name of coast guard (three times).

This is . . . (three times).

Over.

Listen for the working channel in the coast guard reply. Tune to the working channel and pass your message.

Individual Vessel "All Ships" Safety Call: DSC

```
.................
:               :
:  CH70         :
:               :
.................
```

1. Select "All Ships" safety call from the menu.
2. Select "Safety."
3. Press ENTER to send. Do not press the DISTRESS button.
4. The radio will retune to CH16.
5. The screen will prompt you to transmit your safety message.

```
┌──────────────────────────────────┐
│ 37°11.3'N    76°10.2'W   13.20 UTC│
│ SEND SAFETY MESSAGE CH16        ⇕ │
│ REPLY    CH16                     │
│ 366123456       RX           25W  │
└──────────────────────────────────┘
```

```
.................
:               :
:  CH16         :    ▬▬▬▬▬▬
:               :
.................
```

Sécurité, Sécurité, Sécurité
All stations or called station (spoken three times)
This is . . . MMSI number and name or call sign of own vessel (spoken three times).
The text of the Safety Message.
Out.

▬▬▬▬▬▬

Individual Vessel "All Ships" Safety Call: Voice

```
.................
:               :
:  CH16         :    ▬▬▬▬▬▬
:               :
.................
```

Sécurité, Sécurité, Sécurité
All stations or called station (spoken three times).
This is . . . name of vessel (three times).
Text of message—safety issue, position, and so on.
Out.

▬▬▬▬▬▬

Other Calls

Routine DSC Calls

To make a routine call using DSC you must know the MMSI number of the station you wish to call.

1. Select "Directory" if the MMSI is stored or "Manual" if not stored.
2. Enter the MMSI number.
3. Select a "Reply" channel for the response (intership calling only).
4. Press ENTER to send the digital call.

Routine Calls (Voice)

All voice calls made on the radio follow the same pattern and conform to standard radio procedure.

Each initial call has six components:

1. Select an appropriate working channel.
2. Check that the channel is clear.
3. Know the identity of the station to be called. Use the vessel name.
4. The words "This is . . ."
5. The identity of the calling station.
6. Over.

Once contact is established, identities need only be transmitted once on each "over."

Phone Calls

1. From your almanac or coast radio station literature, select an appropriate working channel and listen to see if it is silent and therefore free for use. Note: At the time of writing the service is not planned to be available in all areas for a few years.
2. If you hear the "busy" signal, switch to another working channel and try again.
3. Switch to high power and press the PTT switch for 6 seconds.
4. You should then hear a recording that requests another 6-second key of the PTT switch.
5. Remain tuned to the channel and as soon as the operator is free you will be answered.
6. You reply by giving the call details asked for.
7. The operator will try to connect you.
8. When the call is finished, the link is severed by the shoreside receiver being replaced.

Hailing a Marina: Voice Only

1. Note the relevant details of your vessel: Length overall, beam, draft, and so on, and the number of nights you wish to stay.
2. Select the marina's working channel.
3. Switch to low power.
4. Listen to check the channel is clear.
5. Transmit your call:

   ○ Marina name (once)
   ○ This is . . . your vessel name (twice)
   ○ Over.

6. When you receive a reply, explain why you're calling and give your vessel's details.
7. You will be given docking instructions, write them down.
8. Repeat the relevant information back to the marina.
9. Both stations sign out.

INDEX

Numbers in **bold** refer to pages
with illustrations

A

"A" channels, 34
Admiralty List of Radio Signals, 92,
94–95, 118
alerting system, GMDSS, **109**
All Ships (safety call), 78, 81–82
analog (voice) communication, 2
antennas, about
installation, 21–24, **22**
and portable radios, 11
antennas, types of
emergency, 21, 25
whip, 22
automation for distress traffic, 4, 5,
6, 12, 14

B

batteries, about
care of, 30–31
charge state, determining, 30
and EPIRBs, 114
portable radios and, 11
batteries, types of, 29–30, 31
Boater's Almanacs, 118
buying VHF-DSC radios, 19–20

C

calling another vessel. *See* intership
calls
calling etiquette. *See also* standard
procedure
cellular phones, 96–98
Call Planner, 53, 95
channels, 45–48
garbled calls, 51–52
initial calls, 48–49
unanswered calls, 52–53
watchkeeping, 50–51
working channel, 49
Canada
call sign regulations, 105–6
Coast Guard, 6, 85, 88
MMSI numbers, 17–18
weather information, 92

canceling false distress alert, 71–72,
115
capture effect, 34–**35**
care
battery, 30–31
EPIRB, 114–15
cellular phones, 96–98
CH06, 35. *See also* intership channels
CH09, 36, 47, 49, 50. *See also* intership channels
CH13, 35, 47–48, 50, 51
CH16, 7–8, 36
acknowledgement of distress,
65, 66
calling etiquette, 46–47, 49, 50
coast guard broadcasts on, 84,
85, 90
coast guard monitoring of, 5, 88
distress communications, 58–60,
59, 62, 68–70
intership calls, 79, 83
safety traffic, 76–78, 81
urgency traffic, 74, 75
CH22A, 84, 85, 88–89, 90
CH24, 32, 33
CH70, 36
acknowledgment of distress,
64–65
calling etiquette, 45–46, 50
coast guard broadcasts on, 84,
85, 90
and Coast Radio Station (CRS)
service, 94
distress message, 58, **59**, 62
safety traffic, 76
urgency traffic, 73, 74, 75
watchkeeping, automatic, 4
channels, about
capture effect, 34–**35**
for calling coast guard, 84
and GMDSS, 35–36
International Maritime VHF
Bandplan, 8, 31–32, 44
numbering, 31–32
U.S. Maritime Bandplan, 8,
31–32
channels, types of. *See also specific
channels*
"A," 34
dual-frequency (duplex), 32, 33
half-duplex (semiduplex), **34**